Scholars and Southern Californian Immigrants in Dialogue

Scholars and Southern Californian Immigrants in Dialogue

New Conversations in Public Sociology

Edited by Victoria Carty, Tekle M. Woldemikael, and Rafael Luévano

LEXINGTON BOOKS
Lanham • Boulder • New York • Toronto • Plymouth, UK

Published by Lexington Books
A wholly owned subsidiary of Rowman & Littlefield
4501 Forbes Boulevard, Suite 200, Lanham, Maryland 20706
www.rowman.com

10 Thornbury Road, Plymouth PL6 7PP, United Kingdom

British Library Cataloguing in Publication Information Available

Library of Congress Cataloging-in-Publication Data

Scholars and Southern Californian immigrants in dialogue : new conversations in public sociology /
edited by Victoria Carty, Rafael Luévano, and Tekle Woldemikael.
pages cm.
Includes bibliographical references and index.
ISBN 978-0-7391-7617-7 (cloth : alk. paper) -- ISBN 978-0-7391-7618-4 (electronic)
1. California--Emigration and immigration. 2. Immigrants--California. I. Carty, Victoria. II. Luévano,
Rafael. III. Woldemikael, Tekle Mariam, 1949-
JV6920.S36 2014
305.9'06912097949--dc23
2013050250

Printed in the United States of America

Contents

Preface

Tekle M. Woldemikael

This book is the outcome of a conference focused on the Southern California Latino/a immigrant experience. The conference, "Faceless Latino/a Immigrants: Pathways to Resistance," was held at Chapman University in Orange, California, on March 16–17, 2012. The conference was holistic and interdisciplinary in its approach. It brought together community members and leaders, undocumented Latino/a immigrants, students, activists, pastors, ministers, policymakers, and academics to exchange ideas on the blight of undocumented Latino/a immigrants in the United States, with a special focus on Southern California. The aim was to become more informed; engage in dialogue; learn from one another; and explore new directions on how to march forward, how to make society better, and how to come to a solution that is fair and rational.

Sociologist Michael Burawoy states that "public sociology brings sociology into a conversation with publics, understood as people themselves involved in conversation. It entails, therefore, a double conversation." We aimed for this double conversation in this conference. We wanted our university-based conversation to generate and evolve into what Burawoy refers to as an organic public sociology, "in which the sociologist works in close connection with a visible, thick, active, local and often counterpublic." In some ways, the conference, which aimed for "dialogue" and "mutual education" in a two-day event on a small academic campus, did achieve the goal of organic public sociology.[1]

As an event, the conference created a peaceful, joyful, and even celebratory gathering of concerned citizens and undocumented immigrants who had meaningful, solemn, thoughtful, and reflective conversations with one another. The conference achieved its goal of bridging and crossing boundaries between laypeople and clergy, immigrants and citizens, scholars and students, day workers and families, and people who speak only Spanish or only English. It brought them together, allowing them to share the same space and exchange ideas, often through translations, with second-generation children of the undocumented serving as translators. We believe that we made a small but significant inroad into a new direction on the issue of undocumented immigrants. We wanted the conversation to start at the conference but continue beyond the event, and spread to the larger community.

Our focus was on the sudden public policy debates regarding undocumented immigrants, viewed as a social and political problem whose solution seemed to elude policymakers. These political debates have intensified so much in the last decade that one might characterize the undocumented immigrant issue as the "civil rights issue" of the twenty-first century. Although there are many published works on why it has become a national obsession, this conference was an attempt at breaking the socially constructed barriers and opening up the doors of academia to all walks of life in Southern California. It was an open and inclusive conference for anyone who was interested in the subject to attend, contribute, discuss, and perhaps raise his/her own consciousness on the blight of undocumented immigrants. We also aimed to discuss what could be done about this pressing issue and to come up with solutions at the individual, community, and political and economic levels of society. The papers presented included the testimonials of activists and community leaders; undocumented mothers and workers; scholars and teachers; children of the undocumented; undocumented high school and college students pushing actively to pass the Development, Relief, and Education for Alien Minors Act (better known as the DREAM Act); and lawyers who showed the legal basis for amnesty and more human rather than drastic draconian solutions of deporting undocumented Latinos/as. Understanding the role of media was also the focus of the conference, especially dissecting and breaking down its components so that activists could challenge and change media's vitriolic attitude toward undocumented immigrants.

We wanted the conference not only to have a sober and rational look at the undocumented immigrant question but also to see the human being behind the process of criminalization and demonization of undocumented immigrants. We wished to give voice to local-level solutions. We wished to counter the fearmongering in various areas of American society, including the U.S. Congress, some church and religious communities, and radio and television programs, as well as among some elected government officials. Mass media and some government officials currently give these alarmist voices wide space, allowing them to polarize American society.

We sought to excavate a new understanding on the issue of the undocumented immigrant. Undocumented immigrants are integral to the modern world economy; they are neither a mistake nor a social or political problem. The penetration of capital in many parts of the developing economies of the South (that is, countries located south of the United States) under the trope of free enterprise and liberalization has led to the displacement of small-scale farms. These global forces have displaced people from the source of their livelihood in the South and forced them to move to centers of capital, mostly to major cities and industrial centers in the more developed northern countries, including the United States, Canada, and Europe.

The pressing question has been what the policy of the U.S. government should be toward undocumented immigrants who live and survive in between and among U.S. citizens. Specifically, we wanted to show that regardless of anyone's political will and desires, undocumented immigrants are here to stay. People have been coming and will continue to come to the United States *legally* and *illegally* regardless of the will of the U.S. political machinery for the simple reason that the American way of life cannot be sustained without the day-to-day services of undocumented laborers. The economic foundation of the American way of life is solidly built on the availability of undocumented immigrants who do not have any of the rights of full citizens. The American way of life is based on free enterprise of supply and demand of goods and services. The demand for cheap labor exists; hence, people come to the United States to meet the demand, at huge personal risks and dangers, crossing perilous borders and seas. They would not come here if there were no niche to fill.

This does not mean that they all immigrate simply for economic reasons. Many have social, political, and cultural reasons to leave home. But the overarching rationale for their presence in the United States is a result of the mutual fit of the American economy's need for cheap labor and undocumented immigrants' willingness to work in high-risk and undesirable jobs at low salaries and without benefits. There is demand for the services of the undocumented labor force whose lack of citizenship makes them ideal for hiring in these types of jobs that American citizens typically do not want. They work as maids, home and office cleaners, gardeners, farmers, and day laborers. They provide cheap labor in industries, construction, hotels, and restaurants.

One may ask why they take low-paying, risky, and undesirable work that the U.S. workforce does not want to accept. They endure these jobs because the lowest pay in the United States and other industrial countries of the North is much higher than some of the high-paying jobs available in the developing economies of the South. The income they earn from working in the U.S. economy, however harsh and exploitative it might be, provides undocumented immigrants financial resources to support themselves and their families in the United States, as well as their families in their home countries. Through the income they earn in the United States, many build homes, and support their extended families in the villages and towns in their place of origin. There are also other reasons that force people to seek alternative ways of saving their lives, including political, religious, and ethnic persecution, and lack of safety due to violence from organized crime, gangs, and government forces. Therefore, as long as there is global inequality in income and in political stability between the rich, industrial North (such as the United States) and poor, developing countries (such as Mexico and other Latin American countries of the South), we have to accept the fact that undocumented immigrants will migrate to Southern California.

It is important to look at what is happening at the local level. What are the stories of immigrants? What do communities that work with undocumented immigrants say about their experiences with them? How are Latinos/as, citizens and noncitizens, organizing themselves? What do the pastors, ministers, lawyers, and scholars who serve and interact with the undocumented say and do to counter the assault on undocumented immigration? Politicians and mass media need to understand and question the framing and presentation of undocumented immigrants.

The chapters in this book represent a good sample of what was presented at the conference. However, there is no way to capture on paper the joy, good will, and enthusiasm that all participants experienced. The spirit of the event, its frank and open discourse, and its achievements could not be captured, canned, or sealed into a book. It is not possible for the simple reason that written works need human agency to bring them alive. But this book presents texts that can provide materials for alternative methods and possibilities of bridging communities and breaking barriers between formal and informal conversations, academic and everyday discussions. The chapters should be read as a sample that could be used to open up discourse among interested groups—politicians, policymakers, professionals, scholars, community activists, and students—to explore the issue of undocumented immigration from a humanistic and personal view rather than abstract sociological, political, or ethical perspectives.

We have included two sets of writings: scholarly work and testimonials of community members who share their experiences with undocumented immigrants. On the scholarly side, this book covers the relationship between undocumented immigrants and the intimate political and economic relationships between the prosperous, industrial North and the poor, developing South (Victoria Carty and Karina Macias). It explores how undocumented day laborers find jobs and the risks they encounter in their day jobs (Tekle M. Woldemikael and Ally Noble); the role of the media in framing the issues associated with undocumented immigrants (Chris Haynes and Ivy A. M. Cargile, Jennifer L. Merolla, and Adrian D. Pantoja); and the racialization of undocumented Latinos/as and other youth in school (Caitlin Patler). The second set of writings are by community activists and church leaders, including testimonials of the work done by community and Latino/a activists (Harold Baker); statements from leaders from the faith community, including the Catholic Church (Edward Poettgen and Alexia Salvatierra); and a representation of the voices of undocumented families and individuals and how they are self-organizing to better themselves and live in harmony with their surroundings (Patricia Huerta). And finally we have included summation of the purpose of public sociology as it relates to undocumented immigrants, which is to open dialogue between citizens and noncitizens, and the ivory tower and the surrounding poor immigrant (mostly undocumented) communities, captured eloquently in a keynote address by scholar-faith leader, Rafael Luévano. The scholarly presentation is balanced by testimonials from community activists and religious leaders and laypeople.

We strongly believe that the book could be the engine of change that seems to be lacking at this moment. After all, the call for this conference came from academics' frustration with their detached scholarly analysis of undocumented immigrants' issues and lack of direct dialogue with concerned people, undocumented immigrants, and their communities. We believe our model for a new direction for public sociology, engaging scholars and communities in a deep conversation on undocumented immigrants in small, face-to-face gatherings, could serve as a springboard for resistance against the polarized discourses on undocumented immigrants now prevalent in the United States.

We summarize the main points of the book as follows: First, undocumented Latino/a immigrants are part of the capitalist system and not an aberration nor simply illegal. They are inside of the global system in its reach and its impact. They live in integrated regional economies, stretching from North to South America, tying together the countries of both continents. The regional economies are part of the global economy in which undocumented immigrants are an integral part, occupying the lower position in the hierarchically organized global economic system.

Second, local church leaders, community organizers, and activists have taken the lead in addressing the issue of undocumented immigrants. They are in dialogue with undocumented immigrants and are instrumental in mitigating their difficulties. They are dealing with their hardships in ways that politicians are not aware of. They show that the metaphor of war on undocumented immigrants is not working and will never work, and have methods and ways of dealing with the scary rhetoric about these immigrants coming from some politicians as well as church groups and leaders. They focus on the possibilities improving the situation through grassroots activist solutions.

Finally, we believe that organic public sociology, which emphasizes people-to-people solutions, can solve the crisis. This can happen by allowing greater interaction and dialogue, by engaging in conversations between scholars, church leaders, community organizers, and political leaders with the purpose of treating undocumented immigrants as equal partners in finding solutions. Thus what we need is the conception of global citizenship for all, rather than nation-state-based citizenship that creates artificial boundaries and barriers between people whose lives are intimately tied together through the hierarchically organized global economy. What we need is a conception of global citizenship that recognizes the innate human dignity of undocumented immigrants. There is enough wealth generated in the North through its natural resources and enough labor in the South and North to raise the standard of living for everyone in the global society.

NOTE

1. Michael Burawoy, "For Public Sociology," 2004 presidential address for the American Sociological Association, *American Sociological Review* 70 (2005): 4–28, quotations on 7, 8.

Acknowledgments

The chapters in this volume emerge from an interdisciplinary conference entitled "Faceless Latino/a Immigrants: Pathways to Resistance," held on March 16 and 17, 2012, at Chapman University in Orange, California. Thus we acknowledge and offer thanks to Chapman University's Department of Sociology and the Office of the Chancellor who cosponsored this event. In particular, we are grateful to our chancellor, Daniele Struppa, who offered enthusiastic support and financial aid for the gathering. The School of Law and the College of Education joined our collaborative effort. Our graduate students from the Department of International Studies, Drew O'Neil and Valentina Marinac, assisted us in the planning and executed every detail of this conference. Matthew Hall, administrative assistant in the Department of Sociology, deserves praise for his numerous contributions. Dean of Wilkinson College, Patrick Quinn, supported the conference from its inception and was kind enough to attend and praise our gathering. Patricia Huerta and the community group Padres Unidos brought their grassroots presence and support. We also thank Richard Rodriguez and Georges Borchardt Inc. for granting us permission to publish Rodriguez's poem "Gracias," originally published by NPR. Many others have assisted us in this journey to the completion of this volume; to all we offer sincere appreciation.

Introduction

Victoria Carty

Today, people are migrating at higher levels than at any other time, and the United States is home to more immigrants than any other country in the world. There are approximately forty million people who reside in the United States who were born outside of the country; about 54 percent are from Mexico and Latin America, 27 percent from Asia, and 15 percent from Canada and Europe.[1] Within the United States, more immigrants live in California than in any other state, and of the approximately 10.2 million, nearly 40 percent are Latino/a.[2] Around one-third of these migrants, mostly from Mexico, have entered the United States illegally.[3] While demographic trends speak for themselves (projections are that Latinos/as will account for almost one-half of the population in California by 2050), a vibrant debate surrounds the basic question of what this means for the United States economically, politically, and socially.

As this book goes to press, the U.S. Congress is once again revisiting the discussion of immigration reform. The pros and cons of immigrants entering the United States from south of the border have been vehemently debated for decades and this debate has perhaps become one of the defining civil rights issues of the twenty-first century. In 2006, 10 percent of Americans named immigration as the most important problem facing the country, the highest level in twenty years of polling by the Pew Research Center.[4] Negative attitudes toward immigrants, and particularly toward undocumented Latinos/as, are often rooted in sentiments that cut across dimensions of racism; assumptions of criminality; national security; the state of the U.S. economy; fear and ignorance that often arise from inaccurate or biased media portrayals; and a lack of insight as to *why* many migrate to the United States, even without proper authorization.

These are shortsighted perspectives. For example, despite the myth that immigrants are an economic drain on society, over the course of their lives, both legal and illegal immigrants pay more in taxes than they receive in benefits.[5] Other stereotypes conflate unrelated issues. For instance, although many fear that those entering the United States without authorization engage in high levels of criminal activity and pose a threat to national security, immigrants, including illegal immigrants, are much less likely to wind up in prison than the native born.[6] Though inaccurate, these stereotypes do influence public opinion and result in anti-immigration legislation that has a direct impact on the lives of immigrants.

However, there are groups and individuals throughout the United States that contest these stereotypes and work for social justice for immigrants. These consist of local, regional, and national efforts by faith-based organizations and churches, grassroots networks, and student groups. In fact, the largest Latino/a protest in U.S. history took place in the spring of 2006 when one of the most aggressive anti-immigrant bills was being debated in the Senate and put the issue front and center of the national dialogue.[7]

RECENT LEGAL TRENDS RELATED TO IMMIGRATION

Though rhetorically the United States is portrayed as a country that welcomes the immigrant and makes room for everyone in search of the American dream, the reality is significantly different. It was in the late nineteenth century that the United States began implementing exclusionary immigration policies. What specifically affected Latinos/as the most was legislation passed in 1965 that mandated an evenly distributed quota system of twenty thousand persons per country. This meant that no country could account for more than 7 percent of all green cards or visas for permanent residency. The policy led to the longest wait to attain citizenship status in the world and has been particularly troublesome for individuals from such countries as Mexico, China, and India that have historically had the highest levels of migration to the United States.[8]

As a result, the notion of "getting in line" is not a real option for many who want to come to the United States, and especially for undocumented persons, many of whom are fleeing their country out of economic desperation or for personal safety. Additionally, in some ways, the law itself can be viewed as breaking the livelihoods of immigrants rather than immigrants breaking the law as the regulations are often too complex for those who would like to conform to the legal system but find it overwhelmingly confusing and the waiting period unrealistic. On top of the delay for legal immigration proceedings, there are also lawyer's fees that are required, which many, as they are coming to the United States out of economic despair, cannot afford.

The next major attempt at immigration reform was in 1986. This reform bill regularized the status of nearly three million undocumented individuals, yet it did not deter future entries into the country as the need for Mexican labor, the main driving force of immigration across the border, remained constant.[9] Over the past two and a half decades, the federal government has spent billions of dollars on border control efforts, has implemented hundreds of miles of fencing, has increased deportations and detentions at alarming rates, and has solidified punitive sanctions against undocumented workers, all of which have made the lives of immigrants more and more difficult. However, none of these measures has resulted in concrete results and the U.S. government remains perplexed by the magnitude of the problem.

EXAMINING UNDOCUMENTED IMMIGRATION IN THE UNITED STATES THROUGH THE LENS OF PUBLIC SOCIOLOGY

This volume is the product of a regional conference that was held at Chapman University, located in Orange County in Southern California, in March 2012. It was entitled "Faceless Latino/a Immigrants: Pathways to Resistance." The central theme of the two-day meetings was immigration reform and its theoretical, practical, and policy significance. Panelists and attendees included scholars, lawyers, religious leaders, journalists, students, and community leaders and members. The intent of the event was not only to encourage interdisciplinarity across academic disciplines but also and more important to bridge the university with the local community—embracing public sociology. Public sociology is in part a response to the perception of the academy among many citizens as suspect, elitist, and even irrelevant when it comes to community issues.

It was in 2004 that the president of the American Sociological Association, Michael Burawoy, challenged sociologists to break out of the ivory tower and return to the roots of sociology.[10] What he meant by this was for scholars to take a holistic and interdisciplinary approach to societal concerns. A "public" sociology creates partnerships between scholars and community organizations to work toward social justice. In doing so, it seeks to cultivate strong roots in the community to address social issues and struggles as experienced by local citizens, and to recognize the capacity of all citizens to contribute to the intellectual pursuit of solving social problems.

Therefore, it gets away from what sociologist C. Wright Mills called "sociological bookkeepers" who refuse their role of public intellectuals, and encourages a turn toward what political theorist Antonio Gramsci called "organic intellectuals."[11] Organic intellectuals are scholars whom citizens view as a resource for knowledge and guidance due to their *active* role and assistance in local affairs. They are engaged academics in the community and thus part of the subject matter that they are studying; they do not treat those under study as objects to be spoken about. Burawoy sees this engagement as critical to a genuine understanding of the social reality as lived by others, and he notes that it can legitimate public sociology as a policy-oriented discipline in that it embraces empathy and compassion. It is also a radical departure from the neutrality so often prioritized within the ivory tower; this new approach favors a common understanding and purpose.[12]

In sum, Burawoy, Mills, and Gramsci all worried about higher education becoming a place where intellectuals are gated from the discourse of public values and policies rather than providing a public space and pedagogical outlet that nurtures critical discourse and counter-narratives to those held by mainstream media and political pundits. By embracing public sociology, scholars can enter new areas of inquiry removed from the silos that too often isolate them within the security of their own, oftentimes narrow, areas of specialization. World-renowned public intellectual Edward Said also expostulated the essence of public sociology and the critical role of the public, or organic, intellectual. He did so by rejecting what he considered the sometimes self-imposed political and social indifference among scholars. In a critique of the "traditional" or "professional" roles of intellectuals, and the acquiescence of many of those in academia to these positions, he elaborated: "You do not want to appear too political; you are afraid of seeming controversial; you want to keep a reputation for being balanced, objective, moderate. . . . For an intellectual these habits of mind are corrupting par excellence. If anything can denature, neutralize, and finally kill a passionate intellectual life, it is the internalization of such habits."[13]

In the spirit of Mills, Gramsci, Said, and Burawoy, what this conference sought to do, and what is reflected in this volume, is to give immigration a human face, which is so often overlooked by scholars and policymakers. This book, like the conference, presents a dynamic dialogue between scholars and grassroots voices. Together these voices offer a compelling pro-immigration case that at once is informed and intelligent as well as grounded in the nitty-gritty of the immigration reality. This collection makes a connection between scholarly and public life that combines rigorous scholarship with important social issues, thereby incorporating Karl Marx's quest for integrating theory with praxis.

This text uses an interdisciplinary approach to the subject of immigration in that it strives for knowledge without borders through horizontal modes of the sharing of knowledge. It creates a space where those marginalized and voiceless find a safe environment within which to reclaim their voices. In this way, individuals are capable of linking personal troubles with structural and institutional injustice, thus achieving what Mills referred to as the "sociological imagination" — seeing personal troubles as political issues and new ways of thinking that can circumvent the too common indifference and cynicism.[14] By including community members in this sharing of dialogue, we, as scholars, acknowledge that it is indeed these community members who should serve as the vanguards for providing solutions to social problems because it is they who experience the topical issues on a daily basis that scholars analyze from afar.

OUTLINE OF CHAPTERS

The following chapters make an effort to understand the complex, and often vexing, issues related to immigration by applying public sociology. They do so through both engaging in scholarly analysis and creating space and agency for those most closely affected by immigration. The themes that trend throughout the text revolve around issues related to political economy, the role of the media and its impact on public opinion, obstacles that undocumented immigrants among racialized groups encounter, negotiations of immigrant groups for their sense of integration into mainstream society, and the ways in which community and pastoral reflection and activism rebuke the anti-immigrant mentality and work in solidarity with those exposed to abuses of anti-immigrant dispositions and policies.

In essence, the collection is an attempt to address the multifaceted issues that surround immigration policy and that require a variety of viewpoints in order to broaden the intellectual landscape to best understand patterns of cross-border immigration and the social repercussions. While the bulk of writings on immigration tend to come from a social science standpoint, in this volume, we seek the aid of other academic fields and input from community groups and members. The inclusion of grassroots activists affords a more *human* dimension to the topic of immigration, which is often overlooked by policy-oriented officials and scholars.

Chapter 1, located within a political economy framework, provides an overview of immigration patterns from Mexico to the United States. Victoria Carty and Karina Macias take a step back from viewing the plight of immigrants once inside the United States (the focus of the other contributors) by situating their analysis within a global and historical context. More precisely, this piece examines how international trade agreements and neoliberal policies have negatively affected the Mexican economy, and as a result, have cyclically triggered immigration between the two countries. They reference how, for instance, U.S. foreign policy, international agreements (such as the North American Free Trade Agreement [NAFTA]), the creation of the maquila industry along the U.S.-Mexico border, the militarization of the border, and the War on Drugs have left thousands of Mexicans economically and socially displaced. They are therefore fleeing their country of origin out of financial necessity and escaping the violence of narco-trafficking.

In chapter 2, Tekle M. Woldemikael and Ally Noble offer a glimpse into the lives of day laborers, mainly undocumented immigrants from Mexico and Guatemala, who work in the informal economic sector in select areas of Southern California. They address borders not only in the geographical sense but in the social and cultural capacity as well. The authors highlight the reproduction of inequalities between the first and third worlds in status and identity that migrants experience in the United States, though the physical borders have been crossed. Their piece truly gives a face to faceless Latino/a immigrants, which helps to contextualize, in a real way, the lives of those whom this book is about.

The next two chapters examine the role that media, through its framing and structuring of messages regarding issues related to immigration, play in influencing public opinion and legislation. Ivy A. M. Cargile, Jennifer L. Merolla, and Adrian D. Pantoja argue that while citizens are exposed to a variety of frames on both sides of the immigration debate, it is the *content* of the frames rather than the *tone* that has a greater impact on public opinion when it comes to more punitive measures on immigration. They conclude that the relative weight that media give to different dimensions of immigration has important effects on immigration policy opinions. In chapter 4, Chris Haynes also uses content analysis to examine immigration coverage in four popular mainstream media cable news shows that deal with various topics related to immigration and policy. His analysis challenges conventional wisdom by concluding that conservative media coverage is more complex than often perceived, especially among scholars. Similar to the preceding chapter by Cargile, Merolla, and Pantoja, Haynes's work is in alignment with public sociology because it transcends the academy by promoting and informing public debate on a timely and relevant social issue.

In chapter 5, Caitlin Patler examines how undocumented youth, across different racial categories, negotiate a sense of belonging in a context of legal, political, and social exclusion. She uses extensive survey data to illuminate how certain variables, such as peer and social networks, primarily in school settings, help insulate some of the more damaging impacts of racism and government-imposed illegality status of immigrants. A significant contribution of her research is that it explores new terrain by going beyond the experience of undocumented Latinos/as, which is overly represented in the scholarly research, to include Asian Pacific Islanders and black immigrants. Her exploratory research allows for comparisons and contrasts as to how young people navigate the process not only of racialization but also of legal status as a major accompaniment of this.

The second half of the book consists of chapters that are more grassroots in nature in that they include the voices of those who carry the burdens of immigration status as well as those who work in solidarity with them. Patricia Huerta, founder of the community group Padres Unidos, an organization that has strong ties to the College of Educational Studies at Chapman University, elaborates on how local immigrant communities are working internally to create support structures that enhance the well-being of families and particularly to deal with issues regarding the dangers and challenges Latino/a families face in an oftentimes hostile and unpredictable environment. Her testimony personalizes the predicaments that recent and not-so-recent immigrants face.

Community activist Harold "Biff" Baker writes about local groups positively affecting society, especially within the religious community in the service of education, health, poverty, and gang violence in the following chapter. He recognizes, in particular, the irreplaceable role of the Episcopal Church of the Messiah. This church is located in the city of Santa Ana, California, which is ranked first in the country for "urban hardship." The church, predominantly Hispanic, offers numerous programs to support the community in combating social problems. Baker concludes that these grassroots, holistic, and value-based commitments to the community, rooted in a passionate dedication to imagination and action, are far more effective than top-down and abstract levels of involvement. Community activism, he argues, leads to better understanding of, and ways to address, problems associated with immigration.

The next two chapters focus on the role of pastoral voices in the immigration debate. The Catholic Church and other faith-based entities have long served as mediating institutions between the broader society and immigrants, working in solidarity with those socially and economically displaced and providing a moral voice to the public discourse. The call for solidarity was placed in the national spotlight when, in 2006, Cardinal Roger Mahoney of Los Angeles publicly and unapologetically emboldened priests and parishioners to disobey any law that outlawed humanitarian assistance for the undocumented. Many have heeded the call for humane immigration reform. This type of reform emphasizes human needs over economic priorities, and is critical of walls that physically, socially, and psychologically separate newcomers from U.S. natives.

Edward Poettgen, for example, a pastor at Immaculate Heart of Mary Catholic Church in Santa Ana who serves over five thousand parishioners (almost all Latino/a and undocumented) and a member of a number of community groups, makes a strong argument for humane immigration reform. He interestingly notes that over his thirty-two years of hearing confessions not once has anyone confessed that they were in the United States illegally. In other words, despite the sometimes hateful political rhetoric and negative media attention, the undocumented do not view coming to the United States lacking official papers as a sin or a failure, but as a form of survival to feed their families and dream of a better life for their children (despite the risks of leaving, and the abuses and injustices upon arrival). In chapter 9, Alexia Salvatierra, a Lutheran pastor and member of a variety of faith-based organizations, notes how the participation of faith leaders and congregations, in the struggle for immigrant rights and immigration reform, provides unique resources that include ethical principles, an institutional network for immigration organizing, and dialogue and framework that helps the broader public view immigrants in more positive ways. This, she witnesses, often changes the public debate.

In the concluding chapter, Rafael Luévano, a professor of religious studies and pastor, asks the academic community to "consider what responsibility [it] has for the Latino/a community in our midst." He argues that the sharing of resources through dialogue is critical to common understanding and awareness of the complex dynamics that take place within the surroundings that academics attempt to understand, but often deal with in abstractions. This failure to engage with those under study through vibrant and informed exchanges of knowledge is the antithesis of public sociology and hinders the kinds of networking between academics and members of the community that can lead to substantial and meaningful immigration reform, and one that considers the human costs of contemporary policies. His piece demonstrates, with clarity, the practicality of public sociology and what is required of scholars to engage in such an endeavor.

NOTES

1. Demetrios G. Papademetriou and Aaron Terrazas, *Immigrants and the Current Economic Crisis: Research, Evidence, Policy Changes, and Implications* (Washington, DC: Migration Policy Institute, 2009), 1, http://www.migrationpolicy.org/pubs/lmi_recessionjan09.pdf.
2. United States Census Bureau, "State and County Quick Facts: California," http://quickfacts.census.gov/qfd/states/06000.html.
3. Papademetriou and Terrazas, *Immigrants and the Current Economic Crisis*, 1.
4. "America's Immigration Quandary: No Consensus on Immigration Problem or Proposed Fixes," Pew Research Center for the Peoples and the Press, March 30, 2006, http://www.people-press.org/2006/03/30/americas-immigration-quandary/.
5. Congressional Budget Office, "Immigration," 2013, http://www.cbo.gov/topics/immigration.
6. Eyal Press, "Do Immigrants Make Us Safer?" *New York Times*, December 3, 2006.
7. Gillan Flacos, "Spanish-Language Media Credited on Pro-Immigration Rallies," *Boston Globe*, March 29, 2006.
8. Mae Ngai, *Impossible Subjects: Illegal Aliens and the Making of Modern America* (Princeton, NJ: Princeton University Press, 2005), 27.
9. Leo R. Chavez, *The Latino Threat: Constructing Immigrants, Citizens, and the Nation* (Stanford, CA: Stanford University Press, 2008), 110.
10. Michael Burawoy, "For Public Sociology," 2004 presidential address for the American Sociological Association, *American Sociological Review* 70 (2005): 4–28.
11. C. Wright Mills, *White Collar: The American Middle Classes* (New York: Oxford University Press, 1959); and Antonio Gramsci, *Selections from the Prison Notebooks* (New York: International Publishers, 1971).
12. Burawoy, "For Public Sociology."
13. Edward Said, *The Legacy of a Public Intellectual*, eds. Ned Curthoys and Debjani Ganguly (Carlton, Australia: Melbourne University Press, 2007), 25.
14. Mills, *White Collar*.

I

Contextualizing the Immigration Debate through Public Sociology

ONE

Immigration on the U.S.-Mexico Border

The Impact of Neoliberal Policies and U.S. Foreign Policy on Migration Flows

Victoria Carty and Karina Macias

This movement brings together activists from both of our countries to shed light on the policies that have failed our families, neighbors, and nations. United, we will raise our voices to call for an end to a war on drugs that allows entire communities to become casualties, and we will demand a shift in attention to poverty and the lack of economic opportunity that helps breed the criminality. —Javier Sicilia, poet and leader of Movement for Peace in Mexico[1]

Your life depends on a random stranger who could kill you, will probably disrespect you, and will most likely pay you much less than you deserve. But even those prospects are better than the ones you used to have. This is the life of *los jornaleros*—the day laborers. —Gustavo Arellano, editor, author, and lecturer[2]

Every day, on average, more than one migrant worker dies attempting to cross the border from Mexico into the United States, knowing that he or she will be entering an unfamiliar country and culture upon arrival and under constant threat of deportation—if the trip is successful.[3] Fear and anxiety perpetually loom whether it be in the act of driving, working, standing outside in search of work as a day laborer, walking to the grocery store, or merely being at home with one's family. Additionally, it is an all too common stigma that associates being Mexican with illegality.

3

With the abundance of raids and seizures of workplaces and neighbor-hoods over recent years, often without warrants, children born in the United States have become separated from their undocumented parents at staggering levels. Since 2012, the U.S. government has deported over two hundred thousand parents of children who are U.S. citizens.[4]

Where does this desperation to cross the border come from, and why do so many migrants see these high risks as the only alternative? While most of the chapters in this book embrace public sociology and attempt to refine our understanding of the migrant experience within the United States, this piece takes a step back and looks at the push factors that reside at the global and international level and that have an impact on cross-border migrant patterns. In other words, it focuses on the "why" of immigration into the United States from Mexico, either permanent, tem-porary, or back and forth.

Of particular significance to us in this analysis are some of the unin-tended consequences of U.S. foreign policy and the implementation of neoliberal policies through Mexico's concessions with the International Monetary Fund (IMF) and international trade agreements, such as the North American Free Trade Agreement (NAFTA). Both of these priori-tize, among other things, privatization, deregulation, and cuts in social programs and subsidies for key industries. We also examine how the militarization of the U.S.-Mexico border and the failed War on Drugs, supported by both the U.S. and Mexican governments, have served as prompters for migration patterns. We argue that the prime triggers for immigration from Mexico to the United States are twofold: (1) economic desperation rooted in international trade and work-related agreements; and (2) the explosion of violence due to narco-trafficking and the failed War on Drugs that has taken hold over much of Mexico, especially within border cities.

MIGRATION IN THE CONTEXT OF GLOBALIZATION

Globalization affects many aspects of nations' and individuals' lives eco-nomically, politically, socially, and culturally. The latest wave of global-ization—a large part of it related to the recent digital revolution—has created new and immediate connections around the world. Many view the trends as beneficial for economic growth at the national and regional levels, and personally beneficial at the individual level. For example, po-litical analyst Thomas Friedman is a champion of viewing these process-es, embedded in new technological bridges, as having a "flattening" ef-fect. He paints a picture of globalization as the "fall of walls" and the emergence of a level playing field for citizens in the developing world. In his book entitled *The World Is Flat: A Brief History of the Twenty-First Cen-tury*, he states: "The fall of the Berlin Wall didn't just help flatten the alternatives to free-market capitalism and unlock enormous pent-up energies for hundreds of millions of people in places like India, Brazil, China, and the former Soviet Empire. It also allowed us to think about the world differently—to see it as more of a seamless whole."[5]

However, accounts such as these that perceive globalization as an exclusively positive force fail to address the underlying question of what happens to *human* capital and to acknowledge immigrants as the face of globalization. They disregard how the global economy and its purportedly flattening effect on the world have devastated the lives of many workers and citizens in the societies within which prosperous businesses operate. For instance, while Friedman mentions the success of call-in centers in India, he does not mention the garment industry practices throughout the country where sweatshop conditions provide companies like Wal-Mart billions in profit.[6] Similarly, while the majority of industries along the U.S.-Mexico border, from high-tech companies that produce electronics, to clothing and footwear companies that produce fashionable goods, to car and appliance manufacturers that assemble goods for export, effectively secure massive profits for foreign investors, the working conditions and pay within these industries make it difficult if not impossible for workers to survive. The darker side of contemporary economic globalization is that international decentralized subcontracting arrangements, such as those in the *maquila* (foreign-owned manufacturing, typically located in the border region of Mexico) industry in Mexico (to be discussed more thoroughly in the next section), allow multinational corporations to constantly relocate production in the pursuit of lower wages and result in what is referred to as the "race to the bottom" and sweatshop conditions.[7]

Governments in developing countries that face high unemployment rates, such as Mexico, are desperate for foreign investment and thus cede to the regulations put into place by the investors. Therefore, the seamless whole that Friedman refers to is not necessarily "whole" given that those benefiting from globalization are not entire populations. Additionally, while the borders for trade, investment, production, finances, services, and goods are porous for corporations, there are constructed borders in place that impede the mobility of people. This is the great paradox; the border serves as a gateway for commodities yet an obstacle for people.

In response to assumptions proposed by Friedman and others, sociologist William I. Robinson retorts: "Mainstream accounts of globalization, such as Thomas Friedman's book . . . which sees globalization as a new technological-economic system based on the microchip and driven by an 'electronic herd' of financial investors, are divorced from all agency or power structure. When they speak of globalization as some impersonal force, global elites attempt to reify global capitalism as a reality external to their own agency and interests."[8] The next section acknowledges Robinson's critique and in doing so explores the role of agency in U.S. foreign policy across both economic and political dimensions that have served as an impetus for the migration of millions of Mexicans to north of the border.

U.S. IMPERIALISM IN THE QUEST FOR PROFIT AND POLITICAL POWER

Though a detailed analysis of the history of the relationship between the United States and Mexico is beyond the scope of this chapter, we will provide a brief summary to contextualize current immigration issues on the border region. To situate the immigration trends across the U.S.-Mexico border we can look historically at the political and economic dynamics between the two countries. In the eighteenth century, U.S. internal and foreign policy was driven by the concept of Manifest Destiny, the belief that the United States was predestined to be great and rule all of North America. This is well exemplified through a statement made by Senator Albert Beveridge (R-IN) at a congressional meeting in 1900. He summed up the ideology: "We are the ruling race of the world. . . . We will not renounce our part in the mission of our race, trusted under God of the civilization of the world. . . . He has marked us as his chosen people. . . . He has made us adept in government that we may administer government among the savage and senile peoples."[9]

These "savage and senile peoples" originally referred to Native Americans and would later be broadened to include any group that was not Anglo. This ideology served to justify conquest of new territories across the United States, the system of slavery (of imported Africans), and attempted genocide (of Native Americans) for economic profit. More specifically, in the case of Mexico, this mindset validated the conquest of the Southwest and resulted in the United States taking over one-half of Mexico's territory following the Mexican-American War. This was formally established under the Treaty of Guadalupe Hidalgo in 1848.[10]

While the war against Mexico was justified under the guise of "spreading civilization," the underlying issue was slavery. The illegality of slavery in Mexico prohibited the accumulation of wealth for southern farmers in the United States (though of course this was rarely mentioned publicly). The annexation of Mexican territory subsequent to the war placed not only the land but also Mexican citizens in the hands of the U.S. government. The treaty did grant U.S. citizenship to the people living in the conquered territories of California, Colorado, New Mexico, Nevada, Texas, and Arizona, but excluded voting rights and educational opportunities on par with Anglo citizens.

After early European settlers advanced westward under the precept of Manifest Destiny, the U.S. government disseminated its policy of conquest and economic and political domination to other parts of the world south of its border. Just as businesses and political elites profited internally under Manifest Destiny economically and politically by expanding slavery, annexing land, and having access to cheap Mexican labor, they later did so as a de facto foreign policy. In the late nineteenth century, the U.S. government began employing interventionist policies, financially and militarily supporting coups throughout Latin America, which put unpopular but powerful dictators in charge who were partial to U.S. business interests. This helped the United States maintain political and economic advantages in the region and to secure countries as safe havens for U.S. investors to operate without fear of reprisal from governments or workers. For example, between 1898 and 1934, the U.S. Marines invaded Cuba four times, Nicaragua five times, Honduras seven times, the Dominican Republic four times, Haiti twice, Guatemala once, Panama twice, Mexico three times, and Columbia four times.[11]

These interventionist policies were mandated under the auspices of national security and in particular against the threat of communism. However, the reality was somewhat different. General Smedley Butler, a highly decorated marine leader who was the mastermind behind, and carried out, many of these coups and much of the plundering of Latin American countries attested: "I spent most of my time as a high-class muscle man for Big Business, for Wall Street, and the bankers. In short, I was a . . . gangster for capitalism. . . . I helped make Mexico and especially Tampico safe for American oil interests."[12] The blatant military force would later be replaced by a more benign form of economic and political corporate rule under the neoliberal model.

MEXICAN MIGRATION PATTERNS AS LINKED TO ECONOMIC TIES TO THE UNITED STATES

Part of the irony of the legacy of U.S. policy and the government's interaction with non-Anglo groups, which began with Manifest Destiny, is that Mexicans now stream into the very country that was once part of theirs, and where their ancestors had resided for thousands of years. As the popular slogan goes, "we did not cross the border, the border crossed us." In spite of this history, the U.S. response to Mexican migration has always been dictated by the state of the economy at the given historical juncture. There has always been an ambiguous and often contradictory attitude among U.S. citizens and political representatives toward Mexican immigrants. As the financial standing of the country ebbs and flows, so do common sentiments toward immigrants, and particularly the undocumented who come to be viewed as stealing jobs from citizens during economic slowdowns.

The message of a rather schizophrenic attitude toward Mexican immigrants held by many native-born Americans is "we need your labor but you are not welcome as citizens." In fact, upon entry into the country, most are defined as lawbreakers and criminals regardless of their actual status. It is undeniable that the need for Mexican labor has been essential for the functioning of the U.S. economy, which we will outline next, but in terms of accepting Mexican laborers, there have been circular waves of acceptance and rejection.

During World War I, for example, the Mexican government exported Mexican workers as contract laborers to help ease the labor shortage in the United States at the U.S. government's request. This worked well for the Mexican government because its economy was suffering from high levels of unemployment. As the U.S. economy thrived during the 1920s, the steady demand for Mexican labor continued and workers came both legally and illegally because with such great need for hired hands, employers were happy to hire workers who did not go through the proper legal channels, making it easier for both workers and their employers.[13]

Amid the Great Depression during the 1930s, however, there were mass deportations of Mexicans under the Mexican Repatriation program and Mexicans were accused of taking jobs from U.S. citizens.[14] Many of those forcibly expelled from the country had lived in the United States all of their lives and were in fact U.S. citizens. Of those deported, 60 percent were U.S. citizens or residents.[15] It was the soaring unemployment among white U.S. citizens that resulted in this hostile reaction toward migrant labor and fueled the involuntary expulsion.

In the 1940s during World War II, the U.S. government was once again facing a labor shortage and installed the Bracero program to alleviate the high unemployment rate. This program also helped to sustain the desperately needed production of the U.S. food supply.[16] Under this program, workers were able to freely cross the border for seasonal work under short-term contracts and with no enforced border policies as no tangible borders existed. The post–World War II economic boom in the United States continued to provide plenty of jobs for those seeking them from south of the border. In fact, Mexican workers were actively recruited during the war and the decade of prosperity that followed. And, similar to the situation during World War I, when braceros were in short supply, U.S. growers regularly hired those who came into the country undocumented out of economic necessity.[17]

When the economic expansion of the U.S. economy slowed in the mid-1950s, many migrant workers (approximately seventy thousand) were deported under President Dwight D. Eisenhower's Operation Wetback.[18] With the economic downturn, organized labor blamed the financial hardship on immigrant workers, and U.S.-born workers accused immigrants of being scabs and strike breakers. These sentiments influenced public opinion and the volatile backlash against Mexican immigrants returned. As was the case in the 1930s, deportation proceedings of Operation Wetback were invasive and in some ways inhumane. Under the program, hundreds of border patrol agents and state and local police went house to house checking the immigration status of residents. They also checked for authorized paperwork during traffic stops.[19]

Thousands of undocumented workers and their families were taken out of the country by buses, trains, and ships, far into Mexican territory to hinder attempts of reentry. Despite the aggressive efforts, Operation Wetback was ultimately a failure in terms of stopping the flow of Mexicans into the United States mostly due to the influence of powerful agribusiness interests in Congress that were reliant on Mexican labor. Political officials and law enforcement tended to turn a blind eye toward immigration offenses to appease their wealthy donors. At the end of it all, Operation Wetback had no long-term impact on illegal immigration because the historical need for cheap labor has been so great in the United States.[20]

THE MEXICAN ECONOMY IN THE CONTEXT OF NEOLIBERALISM AND THE IMPACT ON IMMIGRATION TRENDS

On the Mexican side of the border, in an attempt to remedy its own economic crisis during the 1960s, the Mexican government initiated an export-oriented model of production called the Border Industrialization Program (BIP), which was installed to diversify Mexico's economy. One key component of this program was the creation of free trade zones in border cities throughout Mexico.[21] It set the stage for what would eventually become a thriving maquila industry under which foreign-owned and foreign-managed factories imported materials and equipment duty- and tariff-free for the purpose of assembly and then export of the finished product.[22] The end of the Bracero program ten years earlier had led to very high unemployment rates on the border, and thus the BIP was also designed as a mechanism to provide desperately needed jobs for Mexicans living in border regions.[23]

Under the BIP, investors from the United States readily moved in and the region was flooded with U.S.-based corporations that were able to prosper from cheap Mexican labor. This time, though, the exploitation of labor occurred within Mexico rather than in the United States. This did much to benefit U.S.-based corporations but little to boost the Mexican economy or assist Mexican workers due to the extremely low wages that laborers were paid. This relationship led to the "race to the bottom"—the constant threat of relocation of production that puts workers and the host government in a very vulnerable and exploitable position. These conditions, which are based on international trade agreements, result in the extraction of wealth from developing countries to more prosperous ones where investors are located.

The Mexican government's interaction with the IMF in the 1970s also negatively affected the Mexican economy. The IMF is a U.S.-based international banking institution that helps financially struggling countries avoid, or get out of, economic crises. During the global crisis of the 1970s, countries such as Mexico, in dire need of foreign currency, turned to the IMF for financial assistance. However, loans provided by the IMF entail certain fiscal and structural adjustment policies that include privatization and deregulation of critical industries, and cuts in social and welfare programs, among other concessions. In the case of Mexico, these additional criteria involved the further opening up of its economy to foreign corporations, the elimination of trade barriers, and reductions in agricultural subsidies for traditional farmers.[24]

Throughout the 1980s and 1990s, these neoliberal policies continued as the Mexican economy progressively opened up even more to foreign companies in the agricultural and manufacturing sectors, concurrently leading to the restructuring of Mexico's markets and economy. This development in turn created tens of thousands of economically and socially displaced people, many of whom would migrate to the United States for mere survival. It was the passage of NAFTA in 1994 that exacerbated the already difficult economic conditions and wreaked havoc on Mexico's economy. One of the most controversial parts of the agreement was the elimination of Article 27 which had been written into the Mexican Constitution in 1927 following the 1910 revolution.[25] The Ejido (communal land) system guaranteed that certain tracks of land would be controlled by the indigenous Mayan population for local production and could not be sold to foreign corporations. This system was dismantled to make way for foreign corporate-controlled agriculture for export, disenfranchising and displacing thousands of local farmers. Additionally, government subsidies for sowing corn were eliminated by the Mexican government as part of the treaty while U.S.-based agribusiness corporations enjoyed generous subsidies granted by the U.S. government.[26]

The result was that local farmers in Mexico could no longer survive economically by growing corn or other traditional agricultural commodities because of the dumping of cheap corn on the domestic market by large agribusiness corporations in the United States. Small farmers simply could not compete with the mechanized output of U.S. agribusiness. As a result, Mexico's grain imports from the United States tripled from 1994 levels, while real prices for Mexican corn fell more than 70 percent and the domestic market was destroyed.[27] While the access of imported goods allowed for cheaper products to enter Mexico, the subsidies provided to U.S. farmers generated an unbalanced trade policy that drove scores of Mexican farmers to border cities to look for jobs in the maquila industry, or to cross the border into the United States in search of work.

NAFTA therefore served to reinforce the maquila sector that flourished in border towns like Tijuana and Ciudad Juárez. There is now about one billion dollars in trade between the United States and Mexico, and Mexico is currently the United States' third largest trading partner in the world.[28] Juárez has become the world's largest border community and has the highest concentration of maquila workers in the country with over three hundred factories. While these factories (*maquiladoras*) provide jobs for those who are no longer able to work in the agricultural sector due to competition from foreign businesses, most pay less than the minimum wage and workers are subject to unsafe working conditions and hostile treatment from managers.

Free trade zones and maquila industries are indeed a global phenomenon and by no means particular to the U.S.-Mexico border. Yet the impact of such trade policies has had a distinct influence in this region, and immigration patterns are more complicated than many other places in the world because of the proximity of Mexicans to the U.S. border. The option of working in a maquiladora is often a stepping stone for people who then decide to head to the United States.[29]

Since most of the maquiladoras are located in, or very near, gateway cities, there is no escape from encountering people who are coming from or have decided to migrate to the United States. Also, given the border region, the idea of returning to their homeland or going back and forth is always a tangible potential for workers, and for some, the ultimate goal (though this is becoming increasingly difficult). As a result, many Mexicans experience a duality type of existence on either side of the border.[30]

In sum, NAFTA created and sustained the already extant cycle of poverty and migration. Ninety percent of Mexican household incomes either stagnated or declined since the passage of NAFTA, and in 2004 the minimum wage was equivalent to less than four dollars per day in the United States; this is among the lowest in the world.[31] Rather than providing new job opportunities in Mexico, it fueled immigration across the border at even higher rates. When NAFTA was implemented, 4.6 million Mexicans were residing in the United States; by 2013 this number exploded to 13 million, which is 11 percent of Mexico's population.[32] As journalist Juan Gonzalez summarizes: "NAFTA set off a stampede by U.S. and other foreign investors to gobble up key portions of Mexico's manufacturing, agricultural, and banking industries. The sudden infusion of foreign capital . . . drove so many small Mexican manufacturers and farmers out of business that millions of people were dislocated and unemployment mushroomed. Thus, instead of reducing the pressure on Mexicans to migrate, NAFTA increased it."[33]

How would the United States respond to the swelling numbers of migrants, many of whom would be undocumented? In anticipation of this influx, and to try to hinder it, in 1994 President Bill Clinton implemented Operation Gatekeeper, which established a wall in San Diego County, where most crossings were taking place, and militarized the border. The Immigration and Naturalization Service (INS) was put in charge of stemming the tide to "restore integrity and safety to the nation's busiest border."[34] Between 1994 and 1997, the INS budget doubled as did the number of border patrol agents. With easy access routes closed, the use of coyotes (professional smugglers) for border crossing skyrocketed, as did the accompanying rates of kidnappings, extortion, and deaths, as immigrants were forced to cross clandestinely and became easy and vulnerable targets of prey by coyotes.

Rather than quelling the tide of immigration, therefore, Operation Gatekeeper merely forced migrants to cross through new locations and use new ways to enter the United States. This led to serious repercussions that were financially costly for the United States and humanly costly for Mexican border crossers. For example, prosecution for illegal entry or reentry rose from 12,500 in 2002 to over 85,000 in 2013.[35] Currently, immigration-related offenses are the leading type of federal prosecution. In fact, they make up more than 40 percent of cases; many of these are due to attempts to reenter the United States following deportation to reconnect with family.[36] The Department of Homeland Security now refers more cases to the Justice Department for prosecution than all of the other federal crime-fighting agencies, and the U.S. federal government spends more money on border and immigration enforcement than on all other law enforcement combined.[37]

As a result of these aggressive border enforcement measures and intense security, there is an increasing level of difficulty and risk involved in crossing back and forth between Mexico and the United States, and therefore many migrants overstay their visas because they are fearful of attempting to return to Mexico.[38] The wall, therefore, has resulted in a halt to circular migration. In 2009, a Princeton University professor, Douglas S. Massey, in his testimony before the Senate Judiciary Committee, elaborated on the unintended outcome of Operation Gatekeeper. He stated: "From 1965 to 1985, 85% of undocumented entries from Mexico were offset by departures and the net increase in the undocumented population was small. The build-up of enforcement resources at the border has not decreased the entry of migrants as much as discouraged their return home."[39]

THE LATEST REPERCUSSION OF NAFTA: THE EXPLOSION OF NARCO-TRAFFICKING AND THE WAR ON DRUGS

Another international agreement between the United States and Mexico that augmented the economic, political, and social problems within Mexico and provided more incentive for Mexicans to flee the country is the War on Drugs. This joint policy is an indirect consequence of NAFTA; transporting drugs into the United States has become very easy for narco-traffickers as the illicit goods can be hidden alongside legitimate cargo.[40] Given the exponential increase in trade between the United States and Mexico, due to NAFTA, checking every truck, car, or service vehicle is an impossible task for any law enforcement or customs agency. Not surprisingly, the United States is currently the largest consumer of illicit drugs coming from Mexico and has been conducting its own, failed internal War on Drugs for decades.[41] However, little has been done to address the demand side of the equation.

Furthermore, as discussed in the previous section, since NAFTA has undermined the livelihood of growing basic traditional commodities such as corn or beans, there is now a pervasive incentive among peasants to grow illicit crops that garner higher profits. Given the ongoing economic and social crisis in Mexico, and lack of employment opportunities and hope for the future, illegal activities and organized crime have become alluring choices in terms of making money and providing status for much of Mexican youth. This contributes to the failing efforts to curb drug trafficking and has led to escalating violence throughout Mexico, fueled by the growth of drug cartels.

The War on Drugs emerged as a collaborative effort between the United States and Mexico to destroy the drug cartels under the umbrella of national security. In Mexico, the program officially began in 2006 under President Felipe Calderón's six-year term, which has been characterized by many Mexicans as *el sexenio de la muerte*, or the six years of death. By the end of Calderón's term in office, according to the National Institute of Statistics and Geography of Mexico, an estimated 120,000 people had been killed due to drug-related violence.[42] A major reason for the surge in violence is Calderón's lack of necessary resources to battle the cartels through traditional forms of law enforcement; he deployed fifty thousand military troops to civilian areas.[43]

Within three years, Calderón's government had doubled expenditures for security and the number of federal police officers increased from six thousand to thirty-five thousand. They were deployed with the intention of capturing or killing drug lords through targeted assassinations, but ironically resulted in the splintering and acceleration of organized crime. Dozens of new cartels have emerged as turf wars have broken out en mass. The spread of cartels and criminal activity has been accompanied by narco-trafficking throughout much of Mexico. Transnational drug-trafficking organizations have grown more ubiquitous and have expanded into new terrain throughout Mexico.[44]

Narco-trafficking and criminal activity have led to a huge bottleneck for Mexicans legally trying to flee their country out of legitimate fears. According to the U.S. Executive Office for Immigration Review, in 2011, 6,100 Mexicans applied for asylum with only 294, or 5 percent, receiving it. In total, Mexicans accounted for only 1 percent of the total number of people who sought asylum in the United States. A year earlier the success rate was just 1.5 percent.[45] What this demonstrates is that although undocumented Mexicans are often told to "get in line" and use the formal immigration process, the reality is that, between a lack of visas available and Mexicans by and large unable to successfully be granted asylum status, illegal crossings are inevitable.

The stratospheric rate of violence, spurred by the War on Drugs, has therefore compounded a new wave of political, economic, and social destabilization throughout Mexico. Though poverty is perhaps the most recognizable and widely cited reason explaining the explosion of migration rates out of Mexico, violence is another, though often overlooked, driving force. Given these developments, Mexicans no longer leave their country to pursue the American dream and a better life; instead they seek to escape the Mexican nightmare.

This is especially true for the approximately 1.5 million people who reside in the state of Chihuahua. Ciudad Juárez is by far the most violent city within this state and has in fact been labeled the "murder capital of the world."[46] In 2010, over three thousand people died in Juárez due to violence, and nearly 25 percent of cartel-related deaths occurred in the city, despite the fact that the government at times has deployed 25 percent of its forces there. Both the economic and social costs are crippling. For instance, the number of abandoned houses has risen to 116,000 since 2008, a quarter of the businesses in Juárez have closed, and consequently eighty thousand citizens lost their jobs in 2009.[47]

Much of the violence in Juárez is targeted at a specific demographic. Since cartels operate with almost complete impunity, there has been a huge increase of murder of young, female maquila workers, often walking to or from work late at night or in the very early morning hours. As described previously, the lack of work in rural areas in the agricultural sector has led to high unemployment rates; therefore, many men are either choosing to leave rural regions to find work in the United States or to rely on female members of the household for additional (or sole) income for their families. The thousands of random killings of these young women by cartels as a way to mark their territory have been labeled "feminicide." These murders are an example of how the economic hardship brought about by neoliberal policies is accompanied by devastating levels of physical violence and the destabilization of societies.[48]

To address the explosion of violence and drug trafficking, President Barack Obama (who deported more immigrants in his first three years of office than any other president since the 1950s) proposed the Merida Initiative in June 2008.[49] This initiative was put into place with the acquiescence of the Mexican government. Under the plan, Mexico receives money from the United States for weapons to enable the government to combat the flourishing drug cartels. To date, Mexico has received 1.4 billion dollars of the allotted money to train and equip military and police officials.[50] The overall goals include disrupting the ability of organized crime to function; institutionalizing the rule of law and eliminating corruption at the local, state, and federal levels; creating new and more efficient forms of border security; and building healthier, safer, and stronger communities in which citizens feel they have a stake.[51] This initiative, as with the War on Drugs in general, has been a failure so far and has not played a role in deterring border crossings.

U.S. INTERNAL IMMIGRATION POLICY AND THE MYOPIC VIEW OF MEXICAN IMMIGRATION

The U.S. federal government has not been able to stop undocumented persons from entering the country despite a variety of methods that it has used. However, at the state level, some politicians and voters have made concerted attempts to halt immigration, as well as to implement certain measures to make immigrants' lives so difficult that they will either leave voluntarily or decide not to try to enter the country in the first place. Over the past several years, numerous new laws have been either suggested or passed to ensure this.

The most recent trend began in 1994 when voters in California approved Proposition 187, which would have banned all public services for undocumented persons.[52] The bill was overturned by the courts, but two years later, Congress enacted (and President Clinton signed) a number of new laws that reduced legal and illegal immigration and approved other measures that sped up the deportation process.[53] The hostility toward immigrants continued to grow, however, into the early part of the twenty-first century. The "Secure Communities" measure that Congress passed in 2002 and that several states enacted stipulates that state and local law enforcement agencies must cooperate with federal immigration authorities.[54] Under this act, the Federal Bureau of Investigation (FBI) systematically sends the fingerprints of people suspected of being undocumented to Immigration and Customs Enforcement (ICE) to check against its immigration databases. If these checks reveal that the individual is unlawfully in the country, ICE has the authority to deport them.[55] The situation became even more drastic in 2005 when Milwaukee Rep. James Sensenbrenner (R-WI) introduced a bill to the House of Representatives that sought to make it a felony for anyone residing in the United States without papers (in the past this was a civil violation and individuals were detained and deported), and for others to hire or assist anyone who is undocumented. This bill was defeated after massive demonstrations put pressure on elected officials and raised awareness about the issue among the population at large.[56]

The Support Our Law Enforcement and Safe Neighborhoods Act (SB 1070) proposed in Arizona in 2010 is the broadest and strictest anti-illegal immigration measure thus far.[57] It requires that state law enforcement officers attempt to determine an individual's immigration status during a lawful stop, detention, or arrest if there is reasonable suspicion that the individual is in the country illegally, and to arrest anyone suspected of being undocumented. Until then this was the responsibility of the federal government. Twenty-three states have considered similar legislation.[58] The bill also makes undocumented status a crime under state law, and makes failure to carry proper immigration documents a misdemeanor. Police departments could be sued if they do not actively enforce the new immigration laws.

Though SB 1070 was signed into law by Governor Janice K. Brewer in April 2010, a federal judge issued a preliminary injunction that blocked some of its more controversial provisions. Not to be deterred, other states have attempted to pass similar laws. Government officials in Atlanta, Georgia, for example, proposed an anti-immigrant law that would criminalize giving an undocumented immigrant a ride in a car among other things. HB 56, Beason-Hammon Alabama Taxpayer and Citizen Protection Act, Alabama's immigration law that passed in 2011, requires schools to collect immigration status data on their students.[59] In 2007, the Birthright Citizenship Act, supported by over one hundred members of Congress, tried to overturn the Fourteenth Amendment that guarantees citizenship to anyone born in the United States. These laws, as a form of immigration policy, tend to turn people into criminals upon entering the United States while failing to address the root causes of immigration. Ironically, they also do not acknowledge the fact that many migrants are coming to the very place whose government's policies have made their lives unsustainable in their country of origin.

CONCLUSION

Migration and movement have served as key components to the development of the United States since its emergence. In fact, the country is often heralded as "a land of immigrants." However, the concept of immigration and of the migrant has changed in modern times, and the U.S.-Mexico border is now a place of particular contention. Those considered "illegal" or "undocumented" immigrants today were not perceived as such in the eyes of most U.S. citizens until relatively recently.

In this chapter, we have demonstrated that the narrative of the migrant is complex and misunderstood. People are not merely jumping the border for a better life per se, but are escaping dire economic, social, and violent conditions created in part by international policies on both sides of the border. Some policies have been imposed on Mexico as dictated by U.S. foreign policy or international banking institutions, such as the IMF. Others have been implemented with the support of the Mexican government. U.S. foreign policy initiatives, including Manifest Destiny, the Bracero program, BIP, the maquila industry, Operations Wetback and Gatekeeper, and the War on Drugs, make it difficult for immigrants to survive in a globalized world in which they do not have any significant choice or voice.

To fully understand the "immigration problem," we need to examine immigration within a global context with a distinct focus on U.S. foreign policy toward Mexico. Instead of expanding the failed War on Drugs as part of the Merida Initiative and passing internal hostile laws against immigrants, a more holistic approach would call for policies that foster social and economic development within Mexico. The part of Merida that focuses on building sound communities, for instance, may help stop the flow of immigration to the United States more organically and may serve national security interests in both countries as the rise of cartels most likely would be curbed.

Furthermore, the idea that "the world is flat" because businesses prosper disregards the human cost of trade agreements and international financial institutions that dictate policy and create a permanent under-class consisting of workers tied to low-paying jobs. The neoliberal model opens borders and allows for the free flow of goods, services, and finance, but the daily needs of workers and citizens are often an after-thought at best. This is a huge oversight as the border is inextricably linked economically and the United States historically has, and continues to be, economically dependent on Mexican labor.

As it is commonly recognized, Mexican workers make up the vast majority of agricultural, hotel, restaurant, and construction workers; without migrant labor these industries could not survive.[60] Therefore, in addition to suggesting a more humanitarian approach to the "problem" that considers the push factors regarding immigration, we contend that there is a need on a practical front to acknowledge that the United States simply needs Mexican workers. This recognition, in turn, would pro-blematize attitudes that wax and wane in step with the health of the U.S. economy, which we believe are shortsighted. An assessment of the his-torical relations between the two countries reveals how certain interna-tional policies have led to a sense of desperation among Mexicans, who are caught in the crossfire of international policies and bear the brunt of legal repercussions mainly embedded in attitudinal sentiments that go from acceptance at one historical moment to rejection at the next.

As the saying goes for many migrants, it is better to die trying to cross the border than to die slowly at home. This analysis calls on us to critical-ly examine the structural economic and political policies that are in place that deny many Mexicans the ability to meet their basic daily needs. While the media and political pundits typically paint a different picture, the fact is that migrants are merely a symptom of these structural condi-tions that lead to a lack of economic security and personal safety. We see *conditions*, not the people, as the "problem." If the tables were turned, many of those who promote harsh legislation against immigrants and condone the militarization of the border would most likely find themselves thinking differently and perhaps more compassionately. Such an outlook, however, requires a broader historical and global perspective that connects personal troubles to structural conditions. This, indeed, is at the core of public sociology.

NOTES

1. Javier Sicilia, quoted in "US-Mexican Caravan for (Drug War) Peace Gets Underway," The Beckley Foundation Consciousness and Drug Policy Research, August 20, 2012,
http://www.beckleyfoundation.org/2012/08/us-mexican-caravan-for-drug-war-peace-gets-underway-feature/.
2. Gustavo Arellano, *Ask a Mexican* (New York: Scribner, 2007), 227.
3. Fernanda Santos and Rebekah Zemansky, "Arizona Desert Swallows Migrants on Risky Paths," *New York Times*, May 20, 2013.
4. Michael Shear, "Seeing Citizenship Partnership, Activists Push Obama to Slow Deportations," *New York Times*, February 22, 2013.
5. Thomas Friedman, *The World Is Flat: A Brief History of the Twenty-First Century* (New York: Farrar, Straus and Giroux Press, 2004), 12.
6. Ibid., 21–29.
7. For an in-depth discussion of the "race to the bottom," see Victoria Carty, "Labor Struggles, New Social Movements, and America's Favorite Pastime: New York Workers Take on New Era," *Sociological Perspectives* 49, no. 2 (2006): 239–59; and Victoria Carty, "Transnational Organizing and the Race to the Bottom: Labor Struggles and Globalization from Below," *Mobilization: An International Journal* 9, no. 3 (2004): 295–310.
8. William I. Robinson, *A Theory of Global Capitalism: Production, Class, and State in a Transnational World* (Baltimore: Johns Hopkins University Press, 2004), 33.
9. Cited in John Braeman, *Albert J. Beveridge: American Nationalist* (Chicago: University of Chicago Press, 1971), 13.
10. Richard Kluger, *Seizing Destiny: How America Grew from Sea to Shining Sea* (New York: Vintage Press, 2007), 62.
11. Catherine Sunshine, *The Caribbean: Struggle, Survival and Sovereignty* (Boston: South End Press, 1985), 32.
12. Oliver Stone and Peter Kuznick, *The Untold History of the United States* (New York: Gallery Books, 2012), xxxii; and Smedley Butler, *War Is a Racket: The Profit Motive behind Warfare* (Warwick, NY: Round Table Press, 1935).
13. Juan Garcia, *Mexicans in the Midwest, 1900–932* (Tucson: University of Arizona Press, 2008), 102–104.
14. Kevin Johnson, "The Forgotten 'Repatriation' of Persons of Mexican Ancestry and Lessons for the 'War on Terror,'" *Pace Law Review* (Davis, California) 26, no. 1 (2005): 101–29, esp. 118.
15. Francisco Balderrama, *Decade of Betrayal: Mexican Repatriation in the 1930s* (Albuquerque: University of New Mexico Press, 2006), 22.
16. Jason Riley, *Let Them In: The Case for Open Borders* (New York: Penguin Group, 2009), 184.
17. Leo R. Chavez, *The Latino Threat: Constructing Immigrants, Citizens, and the Nation* (Stanford, CA: Stanford University Press, 2008).
18. Riley, *Let Them In*, 40.
19. Garcia, *Mexicans in the Midwest*, 41–43.
20. On Operation Wetback, see Paul Dietz, "Operation Wetback and the Problems Associated with Mexican Migration to the United States," *Rational Immigration*, April 27, 2008, http://www.radicalimmigration.com/content/view/88/1/lang,en/.
21. Chavez, *Latino Threat*.

22. Miriam Ching Yoon Louie, *Sweatshop Warriors: Immigrant Women Workers Take on the Global Factory* (New York: South End Press, 2001), 66.

23. United States Department of Labor, "Wage and Hour Division (WHD): Davis-Bacon and Related Acts," 2011, http://www.dol.gov/whd/govcontracts/dbra.htm.

24. Ibid.

25. Maria Castillo, *Land Privatization in Mexico: Urbanization, Formation of Regions, and Globalization in Ejidos* (New York: Taylor and Francis Group, 2004), 1.

26. Neil Harvey, *The Chiapas Rebellion: The Struggle for Land and Democracy* (Durham, NC: Duke University Press, 1998), 265.

27. Juan Gonzalez, *Harvest of Empire: A History of Latinos in America* (New York: Penguin, 2011), 269–70.

28. Chavez, *Latino Threat*, 271–73.

29. Mike Davis and Justin Chacan, *No One Is Illegal* (London: Haymarket Press, 2006), chap. 14.

30. Ibid.

31. U.S. Department of Labor, "Wage and Hour Division."

32. David Bacon, Rosalinda Guillen, and Mark Day, "The Price of Immigration Reform Is Steep," *truthout*, June 9, 2013, http://www.truth-out.org/opinion/item/16857-the-price-of-immigation-reform-is-steep?tmp.

33. Gonzalez, *Harvest of Empire*, 250.

34. Joseph Nevins, *Operation Gatekeeper and Beyond: The War on "Illegals" and the Remaking of the U.S.-Mexico Boundary* (New York: Routledge, 2010), 3.

35. Human Rights Watch, *Turning Migrants into Criminals: The Harmful Impact of US Border Prosecutions* (New York: Human Rights Watch, 2013), 13, http://www.hrw.org/sites/default/files/reports/us0513_ForUpload_2.pdf.

36. Cindy Chang, "Immigration Cases Make up 40% of Federal Prosecutions, Study Says," *Los Angeles Times*, May 21, 2013.

37. Richard Marosi, Cindy Carcamo, and Molly Henessy-Fiske, "Is the Border Secure?" *Los Angeles Times*, March 10, 2013.

38. Chavez, *Latino Threat*, 16.

39. See Douglas S. Massey, "Seeing Mexican Immigration Clearly," *Cata Unbound: A Journal of Debate* (August 20, 2006), http://www.cato-unbound.org/2006/08/20/douglas-s-massey/seeing-mexican-immigration-clearly.

40. Marosi, Carcamo, and Henessy-Fiske, "Is the Border Secure?"

41. Mark Karlin, "The U.S. War on Drug Cartels in Mexico Is a Deadly Failure," *truthout*, April 8, 2012, http://truth-out.org/news/item/8371-the-us-war-on-drug-cartels-in-mexico-is-a-deadly-failure.

42. Mark Karlin, "Fueled by War on Drugs, Mexican Death Toll Could Exceed 120,000 as Calderon Ends Six-Year Reign," *truthout*, November 28, 2012, http://truth-out.org/news/item/13001-calderon-reign-ends-with-six-year-mexican-death-toll-near-120000%20.

43. Aimee Rawlins, "Mexico's Drug War," Council on Foreign Relations, January 11, 2013, http://www.cfr.org/mexico/mexicos-drug-war/p13689.

44. Karlin, "U.S. War on Drug Cartels."

45. "Mexico's Drug War Refugees Rarely Secure Asylum in United States," *Latin American Dispatch*, August 25, 2011.

46. Lee Moran, "Mexico's Ciudad Juarez Has 3-Year Streak as Most Murderous City Broken in Upset by San Pedro Sula in Honduras," *New York Daily News*, October 10, 2012.

47. Tracy Wilkinson, "Shady Groups Say It Takes Cartels: Some in Veracruz Are Glad," *Los Angeles Times*, October 19, 2011.

48. For a full account of feminicides, see Rafael Luévano, *Women Killing in Juárez: Theodicy at the Border* (New York: Orbis Books, 2012).

49. Andalusia Knoll, "Fleeing His Own War on Drugs, Felipe Calderón Finds Refuge at Harvard," *truthout*, 2013, http://truth-out.org/opinion/item/14761.

50. U.S. Government Accountability Office Report, April 27, 2011, http://www.gao.gov/assets/100/97459.html.

51. Knoll, "Fleeing His Own War on Drugs."

52. Leonie Huddy, Stanley Feldman, Theresa Capelos, and Colin Provost, "The Consequences of Terrorism: Disentangling the Effects of Personal and National Threat," *Political Psychology* 23, no. 3 (2002): 485–509.

53. Gonzalez, *Harvest of Empire*, 199.

54. Ginger Rough, "Brewer Has 'Concerns' about Immigration Bill: Won't Say If She'll Sign or Veto," *The Arizona Republic*, April 19, 2010.

55. For more on ICE, see http://www.ice.gov.

56. Gaspar Rivera-Salgado, "Mexican Migrant and the Mexican Political System," in *Invisible No More: Mexican Migrant Civic Participation in the United States*, eds. Jonathan Fox, Xóchitl Bada, and Andrew Selee (Washington, DC: Woodrow Wilson International Center for Scholars, 2006), 31–33.

57. Rough, "Brewer Has 'Concerns.'"

58. Juliane Hing, "Arizona's Suite of New Anti-Immigrant Bills Moves to Senate," *Colorlines*, February 23, 2011.

59. Elizabeth Summers, "New Alabama Immigration Law Tougher Than Arizona's 1070 Measure," *PBS News Hour*, June 10, 2011.

60. Alana Semuels, "U.S. Farmers, Guest Workers Pay a Price to Stay Legal," *Los Angeles Times*, March 30, 2013.

TWO

"Here I Am Naked"

The Vulnerability of Day Laborers in the Borderlands

Tekle M. Woldemikael and Ally Noble

This essay focuses on the lives of undocumented Mexican and Guatemalan day laborers in Riverside, California.[1] It examines the multiple borders that they cross, including geographic, social, and cultural boundaries, as they live their lives as undocumented immigrants in the United States. They live in ubiquitous borderlands and micro-borders, and they cross these borders repeatedly every day to make meaningful lives for themselves and their families. The informal day labor market in Riverside provides one perspective on these multiple micro-borders and crossings.

Abel Valenzuela, a professor of Chicano/a studies and urban planning, states that day labor markets have increased significantly in the United States in general and in Southern California in particular. "Day labor" is a term usually used to describe "a type of temporary employment that is distinguished by hazards in or undesirability of the work, the absence of fringe and other typical workplace benefits (i.e., break, safety equipment), and the daily search for employment." It is "the practice of searching for work in open-air, informal markets such as street corners or in formal temp agencies."[2] Valenzuela estimates that in the late 1990s there were between fifteen thousand and twenty thousand day laborers, scattered over one hundred hiring sites in Southern California.[3]

The growth of day laborers in the United States is directly linked to the global expansion of market forces around the world. Sociologist Saskia Sassen points out how the emergence of a global economy contributed to the formation of linkages between industrialized and developing countries that were to serve subsequently as bridges for international migration. It should be noted that in the 1960s and 1970s, the United States played a significant role in the development of the global economic system of today. It was a key exporter of capital, which promoted development of export manufacturing enclaves in many developing countries. As Sassen states, it also influenced the passage of legislation that opened the United States and other economies to the flow of capital, goods, services, and information around the world.[4] This globalization of production has transformed the occupational and income structure of the United States, resulting particularly in the expansion of low-wage jobs.

At the same time, there has been a decline of the manufacturing sector and growth of the service sector, especially temporary and part-time jobs in the United States. This has led to a reduction of mobility opportunities within American society, the weakening of various types of job protection, and the "casualization" of the labor market. It is this "casualization" of the labor market, Sassen notes, that absorbed rising numbers of immigrants during the 1970s and 1980s.[5] The procedural difficulties of bringing in legal migrant labor to the United States from Europe and other parts of the world have led to increased demand for undocumented workers from the developing countries of the South who cross borders at "no risk whatsoever to the employers and under conditions that facilitate more extreme exploitations."[6]

Anthropologist Leo R. Chavez contends that the U.S. media and political pundits have succeeded in framing the presence of undocumented immigrants, mostly Latin Americans, and particularly Mexicans, as a threat to the U.S. economy, society, and culture, which he calls the "Latino threat narrative." According to Chavez, the popular press sees Latinos/as as a threat, as invading forces determined to wrestle the land that they consider was once theirs and thus bent on destroying the American way of life.[7] This ideological construct mystifies actual power relations and minimizes the powerlessness of undocumented Latino/a immigrants.

The persons who cross international borders without proper documents or permits not only become undocumented or illegal border crossers but also carry the borders with them. Their bodies become the microborders, the borderland. Their movements from place to place and their interactions with others embody micro-borders and border crossing. They start residing in multiple micro-borders—cultural, linguistic, gender, class, and economic borders—which they have to cross in order to interact with one another and with members of the host society as well as to survive in the new society. These micro-borders include the informal job market in front of Home Depot in Riverside where undocumented workers attempt to sell their labor; day laborers interact with border guards and facilitators in the job market, including security guards employed by Home Depot; law enforcement officers and other agents of social order police the site; and migrants interact with the people in their neighborhoods.

This chapter is based on an ethnographic study of undocumented immigrants from Mexico and Guatemala. It explores the lives of Mexicans and Guatemalans who work and live in these borderlands and the interactions and negotiations of diverse groups of people who cross multiple boundaries. We start with stories of individuals' actual border crossings from Mexico to the United States, followed by the daily interactions of undocumented day laborers in the informal job market; the views of the laborers; and the perspectives of those who are assigned to watch the boundary and maintain social order, including security personnel, police officers, and employees of a multinational corporation, Home Depot. We conclude with a discussion on how the reproduction of borders in the informal labor market provides insight into the reproduction of inequality between the people of the rich, industrialized North and the poor, developing South.

METHOD AND DATA

We draw material for this chapter from ethnographic fieldwork conducted by Ally Noble in the fall of 2003. Noble studied Mexican and Guatemalan day laborers as part of her undergraduate research work for an ethnography and fieldwork class taught by Tekle M. Woldemikael at the University of Redlands in 2003. She conducted her participant observation for three months near and around a Home Depot in Riverside, where male day laborers sought work. She interviewed employees of Home Depot as well as police officers and security guards policing the Home Depot site. The research was centered on a two-block area but includes implications that reach beyond California and the United States to Latin America. She conducted most interviews in English, with a few in Spanish. She talked to a variety of day laborers of different ages, nationalities, and English-language abilities. Noble visited the site eight different days for a couple of hours each time. She also visited the site twice after she returned from trips to Mexico and Guatemala in the spring of 2004. This limited her conversation with her informants to a simple question-and-answer format. Despite these difficulties, however, the information and observations that she gathered are valuable as data and form the basis of this chapter's argument.[8]

THE MAKING OF "UNDOCUMENTED" MIGRANTS

Latin and Central Americans migrate to the United States because of geographic proximity, political and economic linkages, and the existence of established migration networks.[9] The varying economic, political, and social inequalities between states motivate people to migrate and cross international borders, whose function is indeed partly to maintain global inequality. Although sending and receiving countries may have restrictive controls over the movement of people in and out of their countries, it is the legislation restricting the entry of immigrants to the receiving countries, and not restriction of exit from the sending countries, that creates undocumented immigrants.[10] At the heart of the immigration issue, then, is the fact that receiving nations require migrants to have proper documentation or permission to cross their borders.

In a capstone paper for a Latin American studies major, Noble described her experience crossing the international border from Mexico to the United States.

> The pilot announces over the intercom that we are nearing the U.S. border and will soon be safely arriving in LAX [Los Angeles International Airport]. I look out my window to see hills covered with dirt and shrubs. No line indicating where one country starts and the other stops, like the thick black line on maps. Only when I drove from San Diego into Tijuana did the border become real, cement walls and razor sharp fencing guarded by men in uniform and guns. I looked around the plane; most of us passengers were white Americans coming back from vacation. I resented how easy it is for us, as I looked back to the earth where I imagined the Mexican immigrants who risk their lives trying to cross the invisible border into the United States on foot or crammed into the back of a van with no open windows.[11]

In contrast, let us look at the border crossing of Diego, a day laborer, and his journey to Riverside.

> Diego . . . grew up in Puebla, Mexico, and came to the U.S. in 1989 when he was almost 18. He had finished high school and had saved up $500 for the move. To cross the border, Diego and another young guy had someone who was legal in the U.S. help them. He said it was late, after 11 pm, when they got out of the car before they [reached] the border leaving all of their money and belongings with the driver (the man was a legal [resident]). They hid out, and when all was quiet they jumped the fence and ran and hid in the U.S. territory where they had been instructed to wait. The man came [and] picked them up and they were in. He said he got to Riverside at 2 am and met and stayed with his cousin who was two years younger than him and living alone in Riverside.[12]

These two stories of border crossing provide a glimpse of how a person from the industrial North, who has obtained all necessary documents without any difficulty, crosses borders with ease and comfort, while a person from the developing South crossing the same border goes through the border without documentation, risking arrest, danger, and if caught, deportation.

LIFE IN THE BORDERLANDS: MIGRATION NETWORKS

A majority of undocumented workers in the United States come with plans to return home, and can be considered as sojourners in search of economic opportunity. Scholars tell us, for example: "Despite the widespread impression that Mexican undocumented workers come across the border in search of the promised land, [their] *corridos*, or ballads, by and about them celebrate the less hostile, more familiar ambience they plan to return to."[13] Only a few have any desire to remain here as permanent residents.

This idea of temporary immigration by Mexicans to the United States is illustrated by Diego's story.

> Diego has been in Riverside ever since [arriving in the United States fourteen years ago]. The purpose of coming to the U.S. was to work and earn money to save, send home, and build a better life. He first got a job at a fast food restaurant flipping burgers and then it was at a Japanese restaurant where he work[ed] bussing and cooking for five years. He talked highly of his experience at this restaurant and of the people; he pointed in the direction of the restaurant and said it was still open. Next he worked as a TV builder and installer for seven years where he did well and worked his way up to an assistant manager type position. He said that it was very hard to be higher up than his coworkers because everyone wanted these extra responsibilities—having a key and being in charge of opening and closing, etc. After this the company started to slow down; he had to quit and find another job. He was hired as an electrician, installing in new buildings/houses, which is where he is still employed. He said that right now they are slow but will get busy again soon. He said he came here for extra money. His wife does not work, he has two kids in elementary, and I bet he still sends some money home.

From Diego's story we learn that his purpose for crossing the border was to find work and earn money to save and send home, and then return to build a better life for himself and his family in Mexico. Noble describes why it was not easy for Diego to go back.

> Diego has two sisters and one brother who all live in the U.S. They are spread out with one sister in Nebraska, one in Utah, and his brother in San Francisco. His parents are still at home. I asked him [Diego] how often he gets to visit his home or talk to his family. He said he's only been back to Mexico 3 times since he got here 14 years ago, but he talks to his family once a week on the phone. I asked him if he ever wanted to move back. He said yes, he has a house he built there, but that his wife doesn't want to.[14]

As Diego's story indicates, just like the lives of ordinary Americans, the lives of undocumented immigrants are complex.

The description of Diego supports sociologist Douglas S. Massey's insight that massive migration from Mexico to the United States reflects the prior development of social networks. [15] These networks consist of kin and friendship relations that link Mexican sending communities to particular destinations in the United States. The entry of additional migrants, in turn, leads to more extensive networks, which encourage still more migration. The same could be said for immigrants from Guatemala, El Salvador, Honduras, and other Central American countries and the rest of the world.

THE SOCIAL ORGANIZATION OF THE BORDERLANDS

Sociologist Daniel Melero Malpica observes that, on the surface, the day labor markets seem completely disorganized, chaotic, and unstructured. "No clear boundaries exist, no entry or exit requirements are in place, no apparent rules or norms prevail, no status hierarchies are obvious." Malpica argues, however, that "beneath surface appearances there is, at least, an informal social organization that imposes considerable structure on the market. Institutional forms are shaped by the market participants into an organization within which the buyers and sellers operate." He discovered that "like all other markets that persist over time, the one for day labor has developed customs and rules as their participants seek efficiency in their dealing with one another. The rules at the day-labor site are unwritten and are based largely on practice or precedent, but they govern many aspects of the work relationship, including wages. Although not everyone conforms to these standards, they are the recognized norms." [16]

Using Malpica's insights as a point of departure, we consider the labor market as a market with informal boundaries, with entry and exit rules and norms that structure transactions. The rules and norms are, however, uneven and skewed in favor of employers and contractors at the expense of day laborers. We examine hidden social relationships, especially the social hierarchy and inequalities that are embedded in transactions in a seemingly unstructured day labor market. Specifically, we focus on the operation of the labor market as one facet of the larger human experience of the undocumented immigrants who are the majority of day laborers living in the borderland, their interactions with the dominant host society emblematic of the larger relations between the first and third worlds.

Description of the Informal Labor Market

On the corner of Madison and Indiana Streets, near the 91 freeway in Riverside, is a Home Depot where Latino immigrant laborers assemble to be hired for day jobs. Most of the day laborers are undocumented immigrants. They see themselves as day laborers, *jornaleros*, who can be hired for a low price to do a job. The Spanish term *jornalero* means a laborer who works by the day, daily labor.[17] They are widely viewed in terms of their legal status in U.S. society, hence the label undocumented immigrants. Most of the day laborers at this site are from Mexico and Guatemala. The rest are from Panama, El Salvador, and even Cuba and Brazil. The presence of Mexicans is expected because large numbers of Mexican immigrants live in Riverside. The presence of Guatemalans, however, is a surprise and could be attributed to the presence of a Guatemalan immigrant community in Casa Blanca, a working-class neighborhood around the Home Depot site. Along with Mexicans, the Guatemalans live on and around Madison Street in Riverside.

Most of the day laborers speak limited English and all but a few prefer to speak Spanish. At the time of this research, these day laborers varied in age from young men in their teens to mature men in their sixties. The majority of Guatemalans were teenagers, and they were the most recent immigrants. Most of the Guatemalans had been in the United States not more than three years, while many of the Mexican day laborers had made the move over fifteen years ago. Most of these young Guatemalans were the oldest of their family and moved to the United States by themselves or with friends. Day laborers live in apartments and rented rooms, sheds, and garages by themselves and in groups of up to ten; some share houses. Both the Mexicans and Guatemalans send substantial amounts of their earnings home to their families. The reasons for engaging in this work varied among the day laborers.

> For some workers this was their only job and source of income, and for others it was an extra source of income. They came to the Home Depot site on weekends and/or on their off days. Some day laborers came to the site while they were in between jobs or when there was slow down in their current job. There was even a case of one laborer who was seeking political asylum because he was a political activist, wanted in his country dead or alive. He was hiding out there and trying to earn money to do so. There was another case of a retired surveyor who came out there to find something physical to do, although he had another source of income. Payment for the day was something they negotiated when they were hired. The average pay for a day's work was between $30 and $100 at $10 per hour and employers usually paid for lunch of the day laborers. On average, they worked three days a week as full-time day laborers. The summers were high season to find jobs and winters were said to be slower.[18]

As these notes show, some day laborers sought work occasionally depending on other employment opportunities, while others headed to Home Depot regularly as this was their main source of income.

Transactions at the Informal Labor Market

By 7 am, the sidewalks surrounding Home Depot in Riverside are lined with Latino men standing in jeans, closed-toes shoes, tucked in T-shirts, and hats. Here they wait in groups or solo for a car to slow down in front of them and whisk them away for a hard day's work. This location is known as a space for the informal labor market: manual labor traded for pay without taxes or insurance. At the time of our research, nearly 99 percent of the men soliciting day jobs were undocumented, hired under the table and outside of the legal system. Noble illustrates the setting:

> I woke up at 5:45 am this morning to go down to Home Depot in Riverside. I . . . got into my van and on to I-10 W[est]. It was slightly overcast, and very smoggy. The traffic was busy, but still moving fine—no jams or stops. I drove the 10 [freeway] and 215 [South freeway] to the 91 [freeway], exited on Madison St., and then turned left. Home Depot was just a block off the exit, on the left corner of Madison and Indiana coming from the freeway. It is set far back on the lot with the actual intersection corner having a gas station and fast food chain in front. As soon as I crossed Indiana I started seeing Hispanic guys with hats, sitting and standing along the sidewalk. . . . For about three blocks, there were various guys (approximately 7) . . . along the road in groups of two and three walking down toward Home Depot. I turned around back toward the "corner" and past two guys standing, waiting, with paper bag lunch sacks in their hands.[19]

Noble's description typifies the daily sight at this location, as day laborers await possible employment for the day.

Employers and day laborers choose the Home Depot site for understandable reasons. Home Depot, a multinational corporation, prides itself on selling about "40,000 different kinds of materials, home improvement supplies, appliances, and lawn and garden products," which vary from store to store, because it stocks its stores with merchandise matching the needs of a specific area. It has over twenty-two thousand stores throughout the United States, Canada, China, and Mexico.[20] Its customers consist of people doing their own home improvement work, professionals, independent contractors, and tradespeople. Day laborers seek to be hired by Home Depot's customers. Customers often hire them on the spot. Noble describes how day laborers hired on the spot immediately start working to load materials bought at the Home Depot. "A truck came and parked two spots down from me with already picked up workers in the back, who then helped load supplies from a Home Depot pushcart, and then proceed[ed] to pick up one guy from the gas station entranceway corner by just pulling up alongside of [him], rolling down a window."[21]

Day laborers' daily routine generally involves arriving in the morning between 6 and 8 am, either by foot, by bus, dropped off by someone, or by carpool. Some drive themselves distances of over twenty miles. Employers come most commonly in the mornings, and if day laborers have not found work by early afternoon they head home. They are hired for all kinds of labor-intensive work, ranging from landscaping and weeding to construction and painting. Many of the workers are skilled in specific trades and choose work based on their skill set, and younger workers learn from the experienced ones by working next to them.

The episode given next shows how some laborers arrive in trucks and vans and are dropped off at the market. Then they are hired by employers coming by in their cars and slowing down as they look over the candidates. The employers stay in their cars while making a deal with the laborers and hire them on the spot.

> I turned into Home Depot's long driveway and past about three guys waiting. I parked in the middle of the lot. . . . There were two other guys [at the] top of the entrance from the gas station and fast food into the Home Depot lot. . . . A car drove to the two men and the [driver] rolled down his window. One of the standing men went and talked to the driver and then motioned to his friend, and they both got into the car and drove off. I watched the guys standing, waiting; hold their hands up when trucks [drove] in front of them. I saw a man dropped off by a van and another truck dropped off two more Hispanic men ready to work. A couple more guys were meandering over the stop that was now empty after those two workers were already picked up.[22]

This pattern of arriving, waiting, and being picked up for work is repeated throughout the morning:

> I started to feel awkward just sitting in my parked car right in front of the gas station entrance watching everyone so I drove back to the Home Depot lot. I parked in about the same spot. . . . The long roadway to Home Depot had more than doubled with . . . about 8 guys standing. . . . A green-blue minivan started driving slowly down the long entrance road and the guys moved with him, heading toward Madison. Another small blue car came and stopped and about 5 guys ran to it. One or two men were accepted into the car and the others walked back to the side slowly while the car exited the lot. More guys were starting to congregate by the gas station and Home Depot lot. There were two groups of 2 and 3 guys. When I looked back to the roadway entrance there were no more guys standing.[23]

These descriptions demonstrate that the labor market favors the employers; there are more workers competing for jobs than there are employers. Furthermore, hardly any conversation occurs between the employers and laborers, for the going price of labor is known and the specific terms are negotiated quickly and easily.

Not all transactions are under the control of the contractors. One of the advantages of day labor is that these workers have the power to choose the work and turn down jobs that they do not want. Sometimes day laborers reject an offer based on a quick judgment, often due to previous experience with the person and/or hearsay about the person from others.

> While I was talking to Diego, a man who had parked across the street walked toward the group of us. He was looking for workers and spoke in Spanish. All that I understood was that the workers he needed had to have experience. . . . No one seemed to be excited by this man's offer; he was an older man, sixty or so, and a native Spanish speaker. Diego and some others talked minimally to the man and wandered off toward McDonald's. I turned and talked to my seventeen-year-old friends. I asked what kind of work the man was offering. They said painting, which didn't sound too bad to me. I asked why they weren't interested and they just shrugged and said, eh, they didn't like it.[24]

The relationship between day laborers and contractors is complex. Day laborers have at least some control over the type of jobs that they take and can decide for whom they want to work. But more important, there is an unequal relationship between them, with contractors having greater power over workers because undocumented day laborers have no institution or organization to go to in case of exploitation and mistreatment.

Border Guards and Facilitators: Policing Day Laborers

Home Depot is a site that day laborers frequent to find customers, but Home Depot views their presence as a liability. A few Home Depot workers with whom Noble spoke indicated that the store management was worried, because, they claimed, customers complained of "aggressive" solicitation by some day laborers; they also mentioned harassment of some women passing by and concerns about sanitary issues. Initially, however, Home Depot did not see day laborers as a threat. At one time, store management allowed day laborers free access to facilities at the store, including the restroom. Then, the number of day workers started to grow quickly from a handful to over thirty young men. This increase brought demographic complexity to the composition of the day labor workforce and, as one employee put it, "bad guys."[25] The firm established a policy that day laborers would be kept off the property.

Home Depot employees shared with Noble the types of problems that the store encountered once the numbers of day laborers grew. Robert, a Home Depot employee, for example, told Noble: "'We have stuff outside and it started to be stolen and customers would come in and complain [that] things like saws were missing from their trucks. The guys cut a hole in the fence down there (pointing toward the side of the parking lot next to the tracks) and would steal the stuff and put it through there.'"[26] Another Home Depot employee, Sophie, also informed Noble why the store implemented a more stringent policy regarding day laborers on their property.

> She inform[ed] me that the day laborers are not allowed on the Home
> Depot property . . . because of customers' complaints of aggressive
> harassment (day laborers running up to their cars). . . . Home Depot
> had a security guard routinely chase them off the property. . . . I asked
> her if during the winter or when it rained, if the immigrant workers
> ever came inside to warm up or dry off, and she said: "No, they never
> come in here, they just stay out there."[27]

Sophie continued: "'We already called them [the INS, Immigration and Naturalization Service] to come down four times this month but they can only take so many at one time.'"[28]

To protect the interests of the middle and working classes and maintain social order, the city and Home Depot reassigned some security staff and hired new ones, what we call "border guards" and "facilitators," whose task is to manage, control, and discipline the day laborers. Border guards serve as facilitators between the predominantly white middle- and working-class communities in Riverside and the poor day laborers. They interact with day laborers and know about the difficulties of their lives but are also aware of the fears and concerns of the middle class. They protect the middle and working classes from the dangers and risks that day laborers pose to their communities. Border guards are enforcers of the border when it gets blurred or crossed. Thus, they maintain public order without fundamentally disturbing the labor market. Although they enforce the border and share Home Depot's ideology of the border, they also serve as bridge builders between the Riverside community and the day laborers. These border guards and facilitators include police officers who patrol the site regularly, security guards hired by Home Depot, and two Hispanic employees of Home Depot (Sophie and Robert).

When Noble asked police officers if they receive a lot of complaints about day laborers, they said that they have received complaints about solicitations being too aggressive with customers (not contractors) and trespassing on private property around the area. At the same time, they did not try to remove the laborers. The police told Noble that they did not try to deny them from seeking labor or standing, but they want to maintain public order and to make sure that day laborers are off Home Depot's property and not blocking the sidewalk. A security guard reiterated the same points made by the police officers. "These guys have a right to be here and [we] are just making sure they're off Home Depot's property and not blocking the sidewalk, and you know just that everything is okay."[29]

The security guards were hired to keep day laborers off the Home Depot property. Home Depot had three male security guards—Caucasian, Filipino, and African American—working different shifts. As the Filipino guard said, his job was to keep day laborers off the property. He told Noble that some day laborers "steal and harass customers." Furthermore, the guard said, "These guys are not legal and were just here to make extra cash and were hard headed and didn't get it—they couldn't be here." Noble stated that the security guard "spoke English with a heavy accent. He said he couldn't really do much but just tell the guys to leave the property and call 911 for enforcement. He once called 911 twice and the McDonald's once too (it was only 10 am)."[30] It is in the interests of the company and the surrounding community not to eliminate these day laborers, for they also benefit directly and indirectly from the supply of cheap and expendable labor. Home Depot hired security guards and facilitators to keep day laborers off its property but not to eliminate this type of workforce.

Noble interviewed two Hispanic employees of Home Depot for this study. Sophie is a bilingual Hispanic woman who grew up in the Riverside area and had been working at Home Depot since it opened. She is a second-generation child of immigrants, the oldest daughter of Mexican immigrant parents, and has six brothers. Home Depot used her to help deal with the presence of Spanish-speaking day laborers on its property and in the surrounding area. She also served as a Spanish/English translator for the store. Noble also interviewed Robert, whose son John, Noble's friend, told her that his father worked at the same Home Depot where she was conducting fieldwork and would be willing to share his insights on the day laborers around his workplace. In his interviews, Robert showed personal concern and interest for the fate of the day laborers. "I tell them to come to me with any problems, I'm bilingual. I can help and communicate with them. But I really can't help them with most things, most things they know and I know they're on their own."[31]

In their interviews, Sophie and Robert represented their own class interests and the interests of Home Depot. They viewed the day laborers as belonging to a class lower than their own. They saw them as representing first-generation poor immigrants and themselves as second-generation Hispanics who have created stable working-class or lower-middle-class families. They hoped that their children, third-generation immigrants, will be solidly in the college-educated middle class. They saw the history of their own parents in the lives of the day workers. Robert stated:

> It is a catch-22, there's no way up or out [for] these guys. It's not until third generation that good things happen and most of these guys won't make it there. I know this because I'm Mexican, my parents came here and struggled, I'm here and live okay, but it's my kids. . . . [James] who is in college, the third generation who is going to make it, or at least has the opportunity to.[32]

These two intermediaries served between the predominantly white working- and middle-class communities of Riverside and the poor day laborers. They interacted with day laborers and knew about their lives. They were also aware of the fears and concerns of the surrounding community and believed that they could help day laborers avoid exploitation and abuse. For example,

> Sophie was working to get a community center built, a place where laborers and contractors could meet and use it for contracting jobs. According to Sophie, the city council of Riverside had planned to set up a center for the day laborers, but the idea was abandoned because of the downturn of the economy and thus, limited budget for any new programs.[33]

In general, border facilitators act as representatives of the middle and working classes and emphasize the dangers and risks that day laborers pose to their communities. As Sophie explained:

> They litter and leave bottles everywhere, they pee in the bushes, they harass the high schoolers, and there is too much drinking. I tell them that they can't do that, they have to be nice, but they still don't, you know. And they're like an ant problem at our house, once you get rid of them they come right back. . . . Once they get the money they spend it on alcohol and [then] many drunk-driving accidents occur.

Sophie's statement reflects the interests of her class as well as a sense of personal superiority laced with stereotype. When asked about the risks for day laborers, Sophie said: "The risk goes both ways. They can get robbed; not paid or have their money stolen but they can rob too. People who hired them risk getting things stolen. They face being attacked by gangs and are jumped on."[34] For both the employers and the employees, there are potential risks.

Stories of Risks of Living in the Borderlands

These stories of day laborers' transgressions have to be examined in the context of the gross abuse and exploitation to which they themselves are subject. Most day laborers are undocumented immigrants. Working as day laborers enables them to work without obtaining workers' visas, but they risk deportation if caught by INS officers. Despite constant insecurity, the work of day labor depends on trusting strangers. Day laborers face the risk of not being paid at the end of a day's work and being mistreated because of their lack of legal protection. Next, we present eight stories, as told by Robert, a day laborer, and security guards, illustrating the risks and dangers of being an undocumented day laborer.

Story 1: Mugging as told by Robert

> These guys have everything in their pockets. All the money they had earned for the last week or month was in their pockets and the crooks knew this and would steal this, especially the younger guys, and beat them up. They have to save all their money to send home or to find a place to live and they have to secure [a] place to leave anything with

them. The newer guys are very vulnerable and the other guys here are aware of that.[35]

Story 2: Abuse as told by Diego

Three teenage guys came to Home Depot with a pickup truck. They loaded up two guys into the back bed of the truck without telling them anything. "The workers didn't ask or work out where they were going, what kind of work they were going to do, and how much they would be paid. Most of these guys don't speak a lot of English, you know, especially the younger guys so they don't ask." They drove them past Corona up to the mountains, speeding at over 80–90 mph. The workers in the back got very scared and thought about jumping out of the truck, but knew that would be suicide at the speed they were going. The teenagers finally stopped on the side of a dirt road and told the guys to get out and lay down, all three of the boys had guns now. They asked the immigrants for all their money, but the men had nothing. They tore their pockets and searched their clothes. When finally realizing that the men didn't have anything, the teen boys told them to get up slowly and walk away, and if they turned around "it would be a different story." The men started to walk, and then run as the boys fired shots into the air.[36]

Story 3: Labor exploitation as told by Robert

Last week two guys came to them [day laborers] because they have been hired every day for a week and told that they were going to get paid in total on Friday but the employers never came back. The workers wanted [Robert] to help them get their money. "There was really nothing I could do."[37]

Story 4: Labor exploitation as told by a security guard

About three months ago those really big guys, Samoans, . . . had come and picked up guys for work. They had worked for them 12 hours a day for 2–4 days. When the work was completed, the employers asked them for their papers, not have any, they dropped them back off and told them that they weren't going to pay them without their papers, and left the workers with nothing."[38]

Story 5: Deportation as told by a security guard

"A large U-Haul had come to the Home Depot parking lot. Four guys had gotten out of the truck, two from each side and said, 'we need 30 workers and pay $15 ph [per hour].' Of course there was a race to jump into the back of the truck, pushing, shouting, scrambling, yelling. Once they had them loaded up, two pulled out guns and said they were federal officers, closed the back of the truck and left. None of those guys have been back, none of them. I don't know where they took them. I don't know what happened." The security guard said he called INS and they said they knew nothing.[39]

Story 6: Abuse as told by a security guard

One immigrant worker who was picked up from here and hauled all the way out to the "badlands" [Banning, a small town 35 miles away from Riverside, California]. When he arrived, the employer had him get out of the car and asked him for his papers. Not having his papers with him he had nothing to give to the "boss." The employer then told the worker to get the hell off the property then. Trying to be rational, the worker asked if he wasn't going to let him work for him if he could at least take him back. The employer said no and went and got a double barrel shot gun, which he pointed at the worker and again told him to get off the property.[40]

Story 7: Drowning as told by Diego

About 6 months or so [ago], two girls came and picked up two workers; one of the workers had something, kind of like asthma but worse. . . . Both workers were standing by the pool when one had an attack and fell in. The girls were screaming but the other worker would not jump in because he couldn't swim so he said no, then both would die. The other man had people to support; he couldn't risk his life for another. Three days later, the girls came back to Home Depot. Diego said that he talked to them. He said they were quite distraught [because] the man who had [fallen] into the pool was in the hospital in a coma. The girls were trying to find anyone, family, friends, and information on this man who had no identification or papers. Diego said he asked around but no one knew him, he was like so many who were alone. The man died.[41]

Story 8: Beating and killing as told by Robert

[Robert] talked a lot [about trying] . . . to help find a worker that was beat[en] up and killed . . . a long [time] ago. [Robert] was dispirited while telling this story. He said that people had come to him with the ticket stub that was all that was left in [the man's] pocket as the only source of identification. No one knew his family or exactly where he was from beside the state name in Mexico. [Robert] said that he looked and had given as much information as possible to his mother, but that they just didn't have enough to work with and had him buried here in Riverside.[42]

Although dealings between employers and day laborers are ambiguous and full of risks, day workers are more vulnerable than their employers. Differences in class and citizenship status between employers and workers allow employers to take advantage of their workers. Since the majority of day laborers' employers are also Hispanic, racial and ethnic differences play less of a role than class and citizenship status.

CONCLUSION

As German sociologist and philosopher Georg Simmel stated, "the boundary is not a spatial fact with sociological consequences, but a sociological fact that forms itself spatially."[43] In other words, the external boundaries of a nation are reflected in the internal variants or alternatives to those external boundaries.[44] "A border is not simply a line on a map but, more fundamentally, a sensitized area where two cultures or two political systems come face to face."[45] Since it is people who give meaning to boundaries, our research focuses on people within border zones as opposed to the boundaries themselves. It examines the micro-borders that people create as they come together in the micro-borderlands. By using this approach, we can avoid reducing border people and communities "to the images which are constructed by the state, the media or any other groups who wish to represent them."[46] Writer Gloria Anzaldua states that although the actual physical borderland between the United States and Mexico is along the Texas-U.S. Southwest/Mexican borderline, there are other borderlands, such as psychological, sexual, and spiritual borderlands, that are not particular to the Southwest. In fact, "the Borderlands are physically present whenever two or more cultures edge each other, when people of different races occupy the same territory, where under, lower, middle and upper classes touch, where the space between two individuals shrinks with intimacy."[47]

Chavez writes that, for the migrants, border crossing is a period of transition typically marked by ambiguity, apprehension, and fear on the part of the migrants. He argues that border crossing is a transition whose obstacles, trials, and outcome the undocumented migrant does not foresee.[48] Similarly, this chapter analyzes a transitional time and space of ambiguity, apprehension, and fear that is pervasive in the immigrant experience. In the words of Anzaldua, the "U.S.-Mexican border es una herida abierta [is an open wound] where the Third World grates against the first and bleeds." The micro-borders between the United States and Latin America (in this case, mostly Mexico and Guatemala) are transported into Riverside, where undocumented day laborers seek employment directly from contractors and employers. The labor market becomes a borderland, a danger zone, to use Anzaldua's words, "where the Third World grates against the first and bleeds."[49] We shed light on how daily transactions in these mini-borders represent and mirror the process by which global inequality between the peoples of the rich, industrialized North and the poor, developing South is continually reproduced.

This chapter explores the symbolic and physical separation, the crossing, and the surmounting and transcending acts of Mexican and Guatemalan undocumented day laborers in Riverside in the fall of 2003. Most of the day laborers, especially more recent arrivals, spoke little or no English, and for some Spanish was their second language (they spoke an indigenous language as their first language). The essay deals with the social organization of the borderlands, especially its hierarchical organization and the embedded inequality between day laborers and their employers and the community surrounding the job market. It examines the day-to-day operation of the day labor market; its social organization; and the asymmetric relations of labor and employers, often characterized by betrayals of trust, exploitation, and abuse of day laborers. The day labor market gives greater power to the employers and contractors, who take workers in their trucks with the assurance that they will come back safe, though there are many stories of workers being bitten, mugged, taken advantage of, not being paid, and exploited in other ways. Day laborers are in constant fear of INS sweeps and lack of safety.

Finally, the stories also point to the loss of workers' lives and the disappearance of individuals without a trace. These day workers were the "faceless, nameless, invisible, taunted as 'Hey cucaracha' (cockroach)" about whom Anzaldua writes.[50] The borderlands are danger zones, where day laborers feel "naked" because of their vulnerability to exploitation, harassment, and deportation. As Diego told Noble, if he had a visa he would be able to sleep at night and not be scared constantly about what tomorrow would bring and worried about whether or not he would be able to feed his family. "Here I am naked," Diego said, stripped of everything and left with nothing.[51]

NOTES

1. Harold Baker and Matthew Hall have read and edited this chapter and we are grateful for their help.

2. Abel Valenzuela, "Day Labor Work," *Annual Review of Sociology* 29 (2003): 307–33, quotations on 308, 307.

3. Abel Valenzuela, "Working on the Margins: Immigrant Day Labor Characteristics and Prospects for Employment" (working paper 22, The Center for Comparative Immigration Studies, University of California, San Diego, May 2000), 1.

4. Saskia Sassen, "America's Immigration 'Problem': The Real Causes," *World Policy Journal* 6, no. 4 (Fall 1989): 811–31, esp. 814.

5. Ibid., 814.

6. Aristide R. Zolberg, "The Next Waves: Migration Theory for a Changing World," *International Migration Review* 23, no. 3 (Fall 1989): 403–30, quotation on 407.

7. Leo R. Chavez, *The Latino Threat: Constructing Immigrants, Citizens, and the Nation* (Stanford, CA: Stanford University Press, 2008), 2.

8. The names of our Hispanic informants at Home Depot are fictitious and any resemblance to anyone in Home Depot is coincidental.

9. Alejandro Portes and John Walton, *Labor, Class, and the International System* (Orlando, FL: Academic Press, 1981), 60.

10. Zolberg, "Next Waves," 403–406.

11. Ally Noble, "Mi Casa Es Su Casa: Undocumented Immigration from Mexico to the United States" (unpublished capstone paper written for the Latin American studies major, University of Redlands, Redlands, CA, April 18, 2005).

12. Noble, Field Notes, October 16, 2003.

13. Leobardo F. Estrada, F. Chris García, Reynaldo Flores Macías, and Lionel Maldonado, "Chicanos in the United States: A History of Exploitation and Resistance," *Daedalus* 110, no. 2 (Spring 1981): 103–31, quotation on 127.

14. Noble, Field Notes, October 16, 2003.

15. Douglas S. Massey, "The Social Organization of Mexican Migration to the United States," *The Annals of the American Academy of Political and Social Science* 487 (September 1986): 102–13.

16. Daniel Melero Malpica, "The Social Organization of Day Laborers in Los Angeles," in *Immigration and Ethnic Communities: A Focus on Latinos*, ed. Refugio I. Rochini (East Lansing: Michigan State University, Julian Samora Research Institute, 1996), 81–92, quotations on 81, 83, 91.

17. Valenzuela, "Day Labor Work," 310.

18. Noble, Field Notes, October 2, 2003.

19. Noble, Field Notes, September 25, 2003.

20. Home Depot, https://corporate.homedepot.com/OurCompany/StoreProdServices/Pages/default.aspx.

21. Noble, Field Notes, September 23, 2003.

22. Noble, Field Notes, September 25, 2003.

23. Ibid.

24. Noble, Field Notes, October 16, 2003.

25. Noble, Field Notes, November 13, 2003, and October 9, 2003.

26. Noble, Field Notes, November 13, 2003.

27. Noble, Field Notes, October 9, 2003.

28. Noble, Field Notes, December 5, 2003.

29. Noble, Field Notes, October 9, 2003.

30. Noble, Field Notes, November 13, 2003.

31. Ibid.

32. Ibid.

33. Noble, Field Notes, October 9, 2003.

34. Noble, Field Notes, December 5, 2003.

35. Noble, Field Notes, November 13, 2003.

36. Noble, Field Notes, October 16, 2003.

37. Noble, Field Notes, November 13, 2003.

38. Noble, Field Notes, October 19, 2003.

39. Noble, Field Notes, October 9, 2003.

40. Ibid.

41. Noble, Field Notes, October 16, 2003.

42. Noble, Field Notes, November 13, 2003.

43. Georg Simmel, "The Sociology of Space," in *Simmel on Culture: Selected Writings*, ed. David Frisby and Mike Featherstone, trans. Mark Riller and David Frisby (London: Sage, 1997), 137–70, quotation on 142.

44. David Newman, "The Lines That Continue to Separate Us: Borders in Our 'Borderless World,'" *Progress in Human Geography* 20, no. 2 (2006): 143–61, quotation on 151.

45. Américo Paredes, "The Problem of Identity in a Changing Culture: Popular Expressions of Culture Conflict along the Lower Rio Grande Border," in *Views across the Border: The United States and Mexico*, ed. Stanley R. Ross (Albuquerque: University of New Mexico Press, 1978), 68–94, quotation on 68.

46. Thomas Wilson and Hastings Donnan, "Nation, State and Identity at International Borders," in *Border Identities: Nation and State at International Frontiers*, ed. Thom-

as Wilson and Hastings Donnan (Cambridge: Cambridge University Press, 1998), 1–30, quotation on 4.

47. Gloria Anzaldua, *Borderlands/La Frontera: The New Mestiza* (San Francisco: Aunt Lute Book Company, 1987), 3.

48. Leo R. Chavez, *Shadowed Lives: Undocumented Immigrants in American Society* (Fort Worth, TX: Harcourt Brace Jovanovich College Publishers, 1992), xi–61, esp. 41.

49. Anzaldua, *Borderlands/La Frontera*, 3.

50. Ibid., 11.

51. Noble, Field Notes, October 16, 2003.

THREE

The Effects of Media Framing on Attitudes toward Undocumented Immigration

Ivy A. M. Cargile, Jennifer L. Merolla, and Adrian D. Pantoja

As a result of unprecedented growth and presence of more than eleven million undocumented persons in the United States, immigration has become one of the most contentious policy issues facing the nation.[1] Congress's failure to pass a comprehensive immigration bill in 2007 led many state lawmakers to pass immigration bills in their states. Given the lack of action at the federal level and varied action at the state level, it comes as no surprise that immigration issues became a permanent fixture in the 2012 presidential election. Both candidates promised to strengthen security along the U.S.-Mexico border and overhaul the nation's "broken" immigration laws if elected.[2]

The civic discourse on immigration is one where consumers are exposed to multiple frames for and against immigration. Some of the arguments in the media focus on the economic costs and benefits of immigration. Meanwhile, we are also exposed to stories that focus on questions of cultural assimilation. National security considerations have been added to the mix in a post-9/11 world. At this stage, we know little about the effect of these different frames on individual attitudes, or on how such frames affect the weight given to different considerations in the formation of policy opinions on immigration reform.

This essay seeks to examine how different media frames structure attitudes toward U.S. immigration policy. Using an experimental design implemented in the fall of 2007, we seek to tease out the effects of different types of frames, which vary in tone, on support for immigration policies. After looking at the main effects of the frames on opinions, we explore whether frames on immigration change support for policy by altering belief content or altering the weight given to existing considerations. We find that the frames have limited persuasion effects on beliefs about immigration, though they do have an impact on opinions by shifting the weight given to existing considerations.

The results have important implications for understanding how media frames on this issue may ultimately affect reform outcomes. The heavier coverage of negative frames in the media may make the public less supportive of a reform policy that is more progressive.[3] However, if the coverage shifts in a more positive direction, we may find that opinion also shifts in a more favorable direction.

SOURCES OF OPINION ON IMMIGRATION

Much of the research examining public opinion toward immigration identifies a number of individual-level factors as significant in shaping attitudes. Foremost among these are economic considerations or evaluations.[4] After all, elite discourse on the adverse consequences of mass immigration typically couches its arguments in economic terms by suggesting that immigrants flood the labor market, displace native workers, and lower wages, and that they are a financial liability on taxpayers.[5] It is therefore not surprising that opposition toward immigrants is elevated during economic downturns as elites prime citizens into believing that immigrants are responsible for their personal and national economic ills. Researchers find to varying degrees that individuals who are insecure about their financial situation, pessimistic about the nation's economy, and fearful of losing their jobs, and who believe immigrants are a tax burden, are more likely to support policies designed to restrict immigration.[6]

Immigration-induced threats are fueled not only by economic concerns but also by social and symbolic considerations.[7] Social considerations typically measure the degree to which respondents perceive immigrants to be a social threat, for example, more likely to commit crimes, pose health risks, and so forth. Symbolic considerations typically capture an individual's definition of what it means to be an American and whether he or she believes that immigrants possess similar traits.[8] Arguments that mass immigration increases ethnic balkanization are an appeal to symbolic political evaluations by suggesting that contemporary immigrants wish to retain their ancestral languages and cultures, and hence are less American than those who "assimilated" into the dominant Anglo-American culture.[9] A number of scholars find strong empirical support for the social instability and symbolic politics hypotheses.[10]

Immigrant-induced economic, social, and symbolic instability can increase feelings of prejudice toward particular immigrant groups. In political scientists Jack Citrin, Donald P. Green, Christopher Muste, and Cara Wong's study, negative affective evaluations of Hispanics and Asians were among the strongest predictors of opposition to policies aimed at assisting immigrants. Similarly, political scientists M. V. Hood and Irwin L. Morris note that these attitudes significantly influenced support for reductions in immigration levels, while sociologist Thomas J. Espenshade and historian Charles A. Calhoun find that they contributed to negative evaluations of illegal immigration in California.[11] However, feelings of prejudice toward Latino and Asian immigrants may be tempered by increased contact with them.[12]

Finally, each of the factors noted earlier is mediated by select sociodemographic characteristics of individuals. For example, individuals with lower levels of education or in blue-collar occupations may face greater labor market competition from immigrants than high status persons, and may therefore display more restrictionist sentiments.[13] Older individuals tend to possess more negative immigration attitudes than younger cohorts.[14] Being an immigrant contributes to positive evaluations of immigrants generally.[15] Finally, Latinos and Asians generally display more pro-immigration attitudes than Anglos as anticipated by the cultural affinity hypotheses while African American attitudes seem to vary greatly depending on the survey used.[16]

Limitations in the Existing Literature

While each of the studies noted previously have significantly advanced our understanding of the factors fostering and mitigating anti-immigrant sentiment, a limitation of this literature is that few consider how elite discourse and/or different media frames structure immigration attitudes.[17] Clearly, the rise and fall in opposition to immigration is likely stimulated by the political context in the form of elite discourse.[18] One reason for the lack of work on this topic is that most studies have used extant public opinion data, which do not allow a clean test of the effect of different media frames on immigration attitudes. In a survey context, we have no way of knowing which frames individuals have been exposed to.

A better means of exploring this question is through the use of an experimental design, in which the researcher has control over which frames an individual is exposed to. Political scientists Ted Brader, Nicholas A. Valentino, and Elizabeth Suhay implemented an Internet experiment on the effect of a positive and negative media frame on immigration and found that opposition was higher when the frames were discussed with respect to Latino rather than white European immigrants, and when the description was consistent with stereotypes (low-wage jobs). Since their study focuses on variation in the type of immigrant and high- or low-skilled jobs, it does not explore the effects of different types of considerations separately.[19] In their study, political scientists Benjamin R. Knoll, David P. Redlawsk, and Howard B. Sanborn focus on how support for immigration reform varied depending on the terms used to describe those without legal status.[20] Most recently, political scientists Jennifer L. Merolla, S. Karthick Ramakrishnan, and Chris Haynes examine how policy frames influence support for a range of immigration policies, and find that support for the DREAM Act is higher when the word "child" is mentioned in association with the act, while support for legalization is lower when the term "amnesty" is used. However, their study only looks at a handful of frames and embeds them in question wording experiments.[21] We seek to build on this work by exploring a wider range of frames that are described in more depth next. We do so through the use of an experimental design, in which subjects are randomly exposed to economic, social/symbolic, and national security frames on immigration policy.

FRAMING ATTITUDES ON IMMIGRATION

Background on Framing Effects

The news media play an influential role in shaping *what* and *how* people think about an issue.[22] Media can influence what and how people think through framing an issue.[23] Framing refers to the way in which the media organize the facts and opinions presented in a given story, focusing on certain considerations rather than others. The goal of frames is to "act like plot or story lines, lending coherence to otherwise discrete pieces of information."[24] Examples of different types of media frames abound. One classic example is dealing with whether the Ku Klux Klan (KKK) should be allowed to hold public rallies.[25] The issue can be framed in terms of public safety concerns or in terms of free speech. While concerns with public safety might cause someone to oppose letting the KKK hold a rally, thinking of the right to free speech might make people more supportive. Multiple media frames have been presented for our key issue of interest, immigration, which we will elaborate on later.

According to political scientists Thomas E. Nelson, Rosalee A. Clawson, and Zoe M. Oxley, there are three models for how readers or viewers might process mass media information. First, the information might induce learning by providing new information to citizens about an issue, thus resulting in the individual changing the content of his or her beliefs. Second, media coverage may prime an issue by bringing associated beliefs and feelings to the forefront of consideration. Finally, media coverage can increase the weight of certain considerations. That is, media coverage might cause an individual to give greater relevance to certain considerations when forming opinions by making them seem more important than others.[26] We focus on the first and third processes in this essay.

In various publications, Nelson, Clawson, and Oxley argue that media frames are most likely to influence opinions via the third process, of increasing the weight of certain considerations.[27] This means that frames can have an effect even if individuals disagree with the frames. Many scholars have found support for this process of framing across issues as varied as welfare and poverty, affirmative action, AIDS policy, campaign finance, land development, and a KKK rally.[28] Scholars have found more limited support for the first process in which frames actually change belief content.[29]

Immigration Frames and Expectations

Our study looks at five different types of media frames. They include economic negative, economic positive, social negative, social positive, and national security frame. These frames vary in content (economic, social, and national security) and tone (positive and negative). Economic and social dimensions on immigration contain both positive and negative arguments. We chose these two because they are most commonly found in the media and both factors are important in shaping attitudes about immigrants and immigration policy. We added in a national security frame since this dimension has taken on increased relevance post-9/11.

Given the literature on media framing, we expect that some of these frames may have an effect on influencing belief content (the first process noted). More specifically, those exposed to the economic frames may change their beliefs about certain economic considerations related to immigration, those in the social/symbolic frames may change their perceptions of the social benefits and costs of immigration, and those in the national security frame may alter their beliefs about national security factors relevant to the issue. Since social/symbolic considerations tend to relate to more gut-level perceptions, we think it is less likely that the social/symbolic frames will alter belief content compared to the economic and national security frames, where people may be receiving new information, which may then change their beliefs. We expect *stronger* effects when we look at how the *weight* of different considerations varies depending on the media frame that an individual receives. In general, economic considerations should have a stronger effect on policy opinions for those exposed to one of the economic frames (negative or positive); social/symbolic considerations will matter more for those exposed to the social/symbolic frame (negative or positive); and national security considerations should have a stronger effect on policy opinions for those exposed to the national security frame.

EXPERIMENTAL DESIGN

To test our expectations, we conducted an experiment in the fall of 2007 with student subjects. Participants were randomly assigned to the control group or one of five treatment groups: economic negative, economic positive, social negative, social positive, or national security. The treatment groups varied with respect to tone (positive or negative) and frame (economic, social/symbolic, or national security). After exposure to the treatments, we asked subjects to evaluate different statements about immigration and different immigration reform proposals. This design enables us to see how different types of media frames influence considerations with respect to immigration, as well as whether the weight assigned to each factor varies depending on the frame.

Participants and Design

Our study took place in November 2007 in two large political science classes at a public university in Southern California. Subjects were given extra credit in class for participating in the study. With respect to demographics, the average age of our subjects was 19.7, 60 percent were female, and 84.8 percent were born in the United States. Our student subject pool was diverse, with 32 percent identifying as Latino, 30 percent as Asian, 20 percent as white, 9 percent as African American, and 8 percent as other. On political disposition measures, the subjects were slightly left of center in terms of ideology (mean=3.4 on a 7-point scale) and more Democratic, with 51 percent identifying with the Democratic Party. Only 18 percent identified with the Republican Party, 21 percent identified as Independent, and 9 percent stated other partisanship. Given our topic, we also assessed how many subjects had a friend or family member who was in the United States in an undocumented status; 44.5 percent responded in the affirmative. We recognize that our sample is not reflective of the national population. However, our primary goal is to assess the causal effect of the frames on immigration opinions, not mean level opinions. A student sample can lead to generalizable results so long as the general population would react similarly to the frames. In other research that we have conducted on framing of immigration and the effects on political participation, we found similar reactions to frames between this student sample and a more representative national sample.[30]

Subjects were randomly assigned to the control (n=76), economic negative (n=78), economic positive (n=72), social negative (n=79), social positive (n=79), and national security (n=74) groups. While random assignment is designed to ensure that subjects are equally distributed according to relevant indicators across groups, post-study diagnostics revealed that participants were not evenly distributed across the treatments with respect to race/ethnicity and whether they knew someone in the United

States in an undocumented status. To ensure that our conclusions are not affected by these variables, we report the results controlling for them.

Procedures

After being introduced by the professor, we asked subjects to take part in a study about attitudes toward immigration. The first part of the survey asked basic sociodemographic questions and political predispositions. These questions were followed with a news article (or not for the control group) that subjects were instructed to read. After reading the article, subjects completed a short survey, in which they evaluated statements about the effects of immigration, and were asked policy preferences on the issue of immigration.

Treatments

All of those assigned to a treatment group read an article about immigration policy reform. The article was made to look like a real newspaper article on the *Los Angeles Times* online website. The first two paragraphs of all of the articles were identical:

> As recently as 10 years ago, only five states—New York, Texas, Florida, Illinois, and California—were dealing with serious immigration problems. Today, immigration affects all 50 states. According to recent estimates, there are an estimated 12 million undocumented workers living in the U.S.

> There is widespread consensus that the system is broke and needs fixing. Several attempts at bipartisan reform have failed on the U.S. Senate floor. The Senate was divided between members seeking to give some legal status to 12 million undocumented workers and lawmakers who oppose such a move. The reform bill is tabled for now, since consensus could not be reached.

The articles then varied with respect to tone and the types of highlighted issues. In the economic negative condition, subjects read that immigrants take jobs away from U.S. workers, push wages down for those who have jobs, and place a financial burden on state and local governments. The economic positive condition also underscored economic considerations, but placed immigrants in a positive light. Subjects in this condition read that business owners rely on foreign workers, that immigrants take jobs Americans are not willing to do, that they actually push up the wages of U.S. workers, and that they do not place a burden on state and local governments (see appendix 3.1 for all treatments).

The next two types of articles highlighted factors related more to acculturation, history, and society. The social negative condition presented a negative account of immigrants. Subjects read that today's immigrants are not assimilating into U.S. culture; that their children are becoming isolated from mainstream America; and that given financial barriers, they are contributing to social problems. The social positive condition touched on similar themes, but presented immigrants in a positive light, focusing on the social, economic, and military contributions that immigrants have made in the United States.

The final article was mostly negative in tone and stressed the problems that "illegal" immigration poses to national security. Subjects in this condition read that the border is very easy to cross, that failed border security was one of the reasons cited for 9/11, and that more advanced technology and a stronger fence are needed to protect national security. There was no direct positive message that seemed relevant in this condition, so we only focused on a negatively toned article.

RESULTS OF OUR STUDY

The Effect of Media Frames on Policy Opinions

We begin by looking at the direct effect of the media frames on immigration policy opinions. We included a battery of questions on support for different types of immigration policies, some of which have been considered by Congress. Since many of the policy proposals are likely related, we conducted a principal components factor analysis on all of the policy items and found two factors emerge with eigenvalues over 1. We label the first factor "policy negative" since many of the more restrictive and punitive policies loaded highly on this factor. The policy negative variable is composed of questions capturing (1) support for building a seven-hundred-mile fence; (2) increased spending on border security; (3) the hiring of ten thousand more personnel for the border; and (4) the characterization of all undocumented workers as felons and support for their deportation (see appendix 3.2 for wording of questions). We label the second factor "policy positive" since the progressive approaches to immigration reform loaded highly on this factor. The variable policy positive is composed of such issues as (1) allowing undocumented workers to stay in the country if they pay fines; (2) creating a guest worker program; (3) granting amnesty to undocumented workers; and (4) increasing visas for skilled workers.

The distribution of the restrictive and punitive policy preference measure by experimental condition is presented in figure 3.1. Higher values mean support for tightening the border and more punitive policies against undocumented workers. Values above zero indicate support for restrictive and punitive policies, while values below zero indicate opposition to such policies. If the frames have simple direct effects on opinions, we should expect to see higher support for these policies (above zero) in the negatively toned conditions (economic negative, social negative, and national security), and lower support or opposition (below zero) in the positively toned conditions (economic positive and social positive). This should be particularly the case for the frames more directly related to these policies, the social/symbolic and national security frames. What we find is that mean support for these policies among those in the social negative and national security condition are in the direction we would expect (mean=0.081 and 0.022, respectively). However, those in the social positive condition have even higher support for these policies (mean=0.164); thus, they do not move in the direction of the frame. Mean support among those in the control group is also quite high, at 0.116. If we turn to those in the economic frames, we see net opposition to the policies (around -0.2 for both groups) in both the positive and negative frame conditions. These differences across conditions are statistically significant according to an Analysis of Variance (ANOVA) (p=0.096). The results suggest that there is not a simple direct effect between the tone and content of the articles and public opinion on restrictive and punitive policies. Rather, the content of the frame seems to matter more than the tone of the frame to individuals.

A different picture emerges with respect to the more progressive reform proposals (policy positive), which we show in figure 3.2. Here we see differences with respect to content and tone. For example, those in the economic positive condition are more supportive of progressive reform

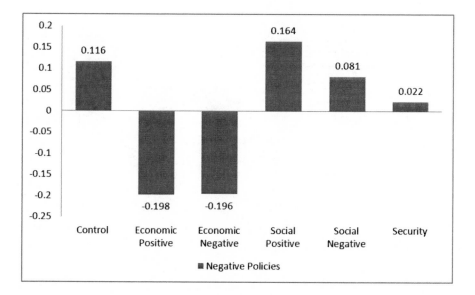

Figure 3.1.   Mean Support for Restrictive Immigration Policies by Experimental Condition

proposals (mean=0.143) than those in the economic negative condition (mean=-0.13). The same pattern emerges when comparing the social positive and social negative conditions (mean=0.044 and -0.114, respectively). The control group hovers right around the neutral point, at -0.01. Those in the national security condition have more progressive attitudes relative to the control group, with a mean of 0.076. While this may be surprising, the article did discuss the importance of a guest worker program. While the ANOVA is not statistically significant (p=0.51), we do find meaningful differences between the two economic frames (p=0.11). In sum, for progressive policy preferences, the frames seem to work in the intended direction, though not all of the effects are statistically meaningful.

While these main effects are certainly interesting, it is not clear what is driving these effects. On the one hand, the frames may be affecting individuals' beliefs about the consequences of immigration, which in turn affect policy preferences. It could be that the frames are more effective in altering beliefs relevant for progressive than punitive policies, for example. On the other hand, the frames may exert effects on policy opinions by shifting the weight assigned to different considerations. In the remaining sections, we consider both mechanisms that may be driving the effects of the frames on policy opinions.

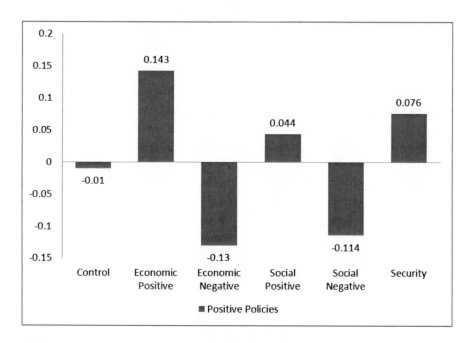

Figure 3.2.   Mean Support for Permissive Immigration Policies by Experimental Condition

How Media Frames Influence Considerations on Immigration

In this section, we explore whether the media frames have any effect on the perceptions that people hold about the consequences of immigration. We presented subjects with a battery of statements about different effects of "legal" and "illegal" immigration and asked for their level of agreement with each statement on a 10-point scale (see appendix 3.2 for wording of questions). One class of statements concerned economic considerations, many of which were contained in the two economic frames. We asked subjects to evaluate such statements as "immigrants drive down the wages of U.S. workers" and "illegal immigrants come to the U.S. to work, not to do us harm." Another class of statements touched more on values, acculturation, and social issues, and some were contained in the two social/symbolic frames, such as "illegal immigration has led to a growth of crime in America" and "throughout U.S. history, immigrants have contributed greatly to cultural, economic, and social advances." Finally, we included a statement about national security, which was contained in the national security frame: "Right now, it is easy for those who pose a security threat to enter the U.S. illegally by crossing the U.S.-Mexico border."

We recoded each consideration such that higher values indicate a more favorable evaluation of immigrants. We had eight statements related to the economy. To reduce the number of questions for analysis, we ran a principal components factor analysis on the eight measures and found two factors with eigenvalues over 1. The statements that loaded highly on the first factor, *Economy 1*, are those that deal with wages and the cost to state and local governments for both legal and "illegal" immigrants.[31] The statements that loaded highly on the second factor, *Economy 2*, are those related to whether legal and illegal immigrants take jobs from U.S. citizens, whether illegal immigrants come to the United States to work, and whether illegal immigrants help the economy.[32] We had six statements related to social/symbolic considerations, and also did a factor analysis of these measures and found two factors with eigenvalues over 1. The two statements on assimilation, one related to legal and one related to illegal immigrants, loaded highly on the first factor, *Social 1*, as did the statement on illegal immigration leading to higher crime rates.[33] Three statements loaded highly on the second factor, *Social 2*, one about legal immigrants reflecting U.S. values, one on the contributions of immigrants, and one on upholding the value of our country as a nation of immigrants.[34] Since we only had one question on national security, we retain it as a 10-point scale measure and label it *Security Risk*. All five measures are coded such that higher values mean more positive assessments of the impact of legal and illegal immigration.

We ran multiple regression analyses on all five measures. As independent variables, we included dummy variables for each experimental condition, and controls for race and ethnicity and whether the person knows someone in the United States in an undocumented status, since the latter two measures were unevenly distributed across experimental conditions. The results for the two economic measures are presented in the first two data columns in table 3.1. For the first set of economic considerations, *Economy 1*, we do not find any effect of the economic conditions on be-liefs. However, if we turn to the results for the second set of economic considerations, *Economy 2*, we find that the economic positive article causes subjects to move .376 units on the factor, which is quite substan-tial. Thus, individuals in this condition were more likely to believe that immigrants come to the United States to work and help the economy. The coefficient for this condition is also significantly higher than the coeffi-cient for the economic negative condition (p=.056 for a test of the equality between the two coefficients). The effect of the economic negative condi-tion is not significantly different from the control (p=.19); thus, it did not have any effect on belief content. These mixed findings for the effects of the frames on belief content fit in with existing scholarship on framing. It also appears that there was some effect of the noneconomic articles on economic beliefs. Individuals in the social positive condition became more negative with respect to the costs of immigration to wages and government (*Economy 1*), and more positive with respect to evaluations of immigrants coming to the United States to primarily work and help the economy (*Economy 2*). The national security condition also had posi-tive effects on *Economy 2*.

If we turn to the social/symbolic belief measures in table 3.1, we do not find any effects of the social/symbolic frames, or any of the other frames, on belief content. As we argued earlier, this is not surprising since individuals likely possess strong predispositions on these dimen-sions, making it harder to persuade them to change their beliefs. Turning to security risk perceptions, individuals in the national security condition are more likely to agree that it is easy for those who pose a security threat to cross the border illegally than those in the control group, though this effect is not statistically significant (p=.228). The only significant condi-tion is the social negative condition, even though this dimension was not mentioned in the frame, and it appears that individuals react against the tone, perceiving immigrants as less of a security risk.

Overall, we do not find many instances of the frames directly affecting considerations. The only effects we obtain are for economic considera-tions. Weak effects on learning are consistent with the arguments made by scholars in the framing literature. The areas where we do not find effects are also those in which individuals likely hold well-formed con-siderations, and thus should be harder to move. Meanwhile, it is conceiv-able that individuals learned more information that they did not know from the economic positive condition, since this story is less covered in the media. Turning back to figures 3.1 and 3.2, individuals in this condi-

Table 3.1.   Effect of Media Frames on Considerations

	Economy 1	Economy 2	Social 1	Social 2	Security Risk
	Coef (SE)	Coef (SE)	Coef (SE)	Coef (SE)	Coef (SE)
Economic Positive (frame)	0.133 (0.153)	0.376** (0.157)	-0.009 (0.159)	-0.078 (0.164)	-0.187 (0.410)
Economic Negative (frame)	-0.066 (0.151)	0.204 (0.154)	-0.004 (0.157)	-0.064 (0.162)	-0.215 (0.405)
Social Positive (frame)	-0.263* (0.149)	0.262* (0.153)	-0.139 (0.154)	-0.119 (0.159)	-0.580 (0.399)
Social Negative (frame)	0.002 (0.149)	0.137 (0.153)	-0.064 (0.155)	0.025 (0.160)	-0.668* (0.400)
National Security (frame)	-0.183 (0.153)	0.547** (0.156)	0.011 (0.158)	-0.031 (0.163)	-0.491 (0.407)
Latino	0.858** (0.127)	0.865** (0.130)	0.775** (0.133)	0.563** (0.137)	2.058** (0.341)
Asian	0.123 (0.123)	0.385** (0.125)	0.233* (0.127)	0.244* (0.131)	0.244 (0.327)
Black	-0.074 (0.172)	0.481** (0.176)	0.361** (0.178)	0.127 (0.183)	0.284 (0.258)
Other	0.396** (0.177)	0.596** (0.181)	0.237 (0.187)	0.489** (0.192)	0.238 (0.476)
Relative/Friend undocumented	0.137 (0.096)	0.059 (0.098)	0.112 (0.101)	0.036 (0.104)	-0.057 (0.259)
Constant	-0.328** (0.139)	-0.757** (0.142)	-0.375** (0.144)	-0.269* (0.148)	3.710** (0.370)
N	449	449	450	450	453
R Squared	0.182	0.146	0.108	0.052	0.119

*p<.10 (two-tailed) ** p<0.05

tion were among those most opposed to punitive policies and most supportive of progressive reforms. Thus, changes in belief content may have at least been relevant in this condition. Even if the other frames did not have direct effects on the expected considerations, they may work indirectly by activating the effect of relevant considerations on policy preferences toward immigration. We turn to this question in the next section.

How Frames Affect the Weight of Existing Considerations

What might account for the different effects across the other conditions if the frames had limited effects on one's beliefs about the consequences of immigration? As we argued earlier, the frames may exert effects by shifting the weight assigned to different considerations. To test this possibility, we ran a regression on the two policy measures, policy negative and policy positive, including as independent variables the two economic considerations (*Economy 1* and *Economy 2*), the two social considerations (*Social 1* and *Social 2*), and the *Security Risk* consideration. We also controlled for feelings toward legal and illegal immigrants, since affective evaluations may influence policy opinions, and race/ethnicity and knowing those who are undocumented. To test the relative weight of each independent variable on attitudes, we ran the regression separately depending on the experimental condition to which the person was exposed. Since we expected that the weight of different considerations would depend on content, rather than tone, we combined the two economic conditions (economic positive and economic negative) together and the two social conditions together (social positive and social negative). Thus, we ran the regression separately for four different samples: those in the control group, those in one of the economic frame conditions, those in one of the social frame conditions, and those in the national security frame condition. We expected the weight of the two economic considerations, *Economy 1* and *Economy 2*, to be higher among those in the economic frame conditions (economic positive and economic negative) relative to those in the control group. Similarly, the weight of the *Security Risk* measure should be higher among those in the national security condition relative to the control group. The weight of the two social considerations (*Social 1* and *Social 2*) should be higher among those in the social frame conditions (social positive and social negative) relative to those in the control group. The results for policy negative measures are presented in table 3.2.

If we first compare those who received an economic frame (column labeled "Economy") to those in the control group (column labeled "Control"), we see that economic considerations are only relevant for those who received an economic frame. The two economic consideration measures are just outside of traditional significance levels in the control group (p=0.13 for *Economy 1* and p=0.12 for *Economy 2*), while they are significant among those who received an economic frame. Individuals with more positive assessments of the economic contributions of immigrants are less supportive of restrictive and punitive policies. These results are in line with expectations. In addition to the two economic consideration measures, both social consideration measures, *Social 1* and *Social 2*, predict positions on the negative policy among those in the economic frame conditions, as do feelings toward "illegal" immigrants. Thus, those who think immigrants are assimilating and making important contributions are less supportive of restrictive policies, as are those who feel more warmly toward "illegal" immigrants.

Table 3.2.   Regression on Support for Negative Policy

Frames →	Control	Economy (positive & negative frame)	Social (positive & negative frame)	National Security
Independent Variables ↓	Coef (SE)	Coef (SE)	Coef (SE)	Coef (SE)
Economy 1 (considerations)	-0.222 (0.148)	-0.221** (0.093)	-0.226** (0.086)	0.032 (0.184)
Economy 2 (considerations)	-0.185 (0.117)	-0.135* (0.117)	-0.179* (0.074)	-0.066 (0.103)
Social 1 (considerations)	-0.159 (0.160)	-0.290** (0.082)	-0.170** (0.076)	-0.354** (0.137)
Social 2 (considerations)	-0.174 (0.114)	-0.128* (0.070)	-0.054 (0.076)	-0.226** (0.105)
Security Risk (consideration)	-0.061 (0.053)	-0.021 (0.027)	-0.081 (0.027)	-0.166** (0.045)
Feelings Legal	-0.021 (0.049)	0.044 (0.034)	0.041 (0.034)	-0.078 (0.049)
Feelings Illegal	-0.050 (0.060)	-0.103** (0.031)	-0.080** (0.031)	-0.020 (0.049)
Latino	0.184 (0.356)	0.193 (0.205)	0.137 (0.194)	-0.003 (0.287)
Asian	-0.040 (0.280)	-0.064 (0.182)	0.325* (0.167)	0.150 (0.271)
Black	0.510 (0.420)	0.181 (0.263)	0.199 (0.237)	0.445 (0.336)
Other	0.318 (0.384)	-0.160 (0.275)	0.115 (0.245)	-0.487 (0.431)
Relative/Friend undocumented	-0.227 (0.256)	-0.189 (0.130)	-0.019 (0.135)	-0.110 (0.194)
Constant	0.748 (0.466)	0.274 (0.324)	0.349 (0.335)	1.485** (0.460)
N	71	139	150	70
R Squared	0.492	0.554	0.537	0.571

*p<.10 (two-tailed) ** p<0.05

Next we compare those exposed to one of the social frame conditions (column labeled "Social") to those in the control group. We find that the first social consideration measure (*Social 1*), related to assimilation, matters for the former and does not matter for the latter. The second social consideration measure is outside of traditional significance levels in the control group (p=0.13), and it is not significant among those in the social frame conditions. This lends support again to our expectation that those who received a social frame would weight social considerations more heavily in their immigration policy attitudes compared to those in the control group. In addition to the first social consideration, the two economic considerations (*Economy 1* and *Economy 2*) influence opinions among those exposed to one of the social frames, as do feelings toward "illegal" immigrants.[35]

Finally, if we turn to those in the national security condition (column labeled "National Security"), we find that the *Security Risk* measure is significant; thus, individuals who thought that it is not easy to cross the border were less supportive of restrictive policies. The results here are in line with expectations in that the *Security Risk* measure is only relevant for those exposed to the national security frame. The two social considerations, *Social 1* and *Social 2*, are also relevant in this condition. In sum, across all three frames, we find that individuals give more weight to considerations relevant to that frame in forming their immigration policy opinions relative to individuals in the control group.

The results for the policy positive dependent variable are presented in table 3.3. For this dependent variable, we should see that considerations have a positive effect on policy attitudes. If we first compare those in an economic frame (column labeled "Economy") to those in the control group (column labeled "Control"), we find that the second economic consideration, *Economy 2*, is only significant for those in an economic frame and not in the control group, while the first economic factor, *Economy 1*, is just outside of conventional statistical levels (p=0.16) for those in the economic frame, and is not significant among those in the control group. We get stronger findings in this case in that it is only beliefs about the economic effects of immigration that influence policy attitudes that deal with amnesty, a guest worker program, and visas for skilled workers among those in the economic frame conditions.

If we now turn to those in a social frame (column labeled "Social"), we find that the second social factor (*Social 2*), dealing with the contributions of immigrants, is significant and positive. While the second social consideration measure is also significant among those in the control group, the size of the coefficient is much higher for those in the social frame conditions, 0.433, compared to those in the control group, 0.286. In addition to *Social 2*, we find that warmer feelings toward "illegal" immigrants increase support for more progressive policy reforms, as do positive economic considerations (*Economy 2*).[36]

Finally, we again find support for our expectations among those in the national security frame in that the *Security Risk* measure is only significant among those in this condition (last data column). The only other measures that matter for those in this treatment are feelings toward legal

Table 3.3.   Regression on Support for Positive Policy

Frames → Variables ↓	Control	Economy (positive & negative frame)	Social (positive & negative frame	Security
	Coef. (SE)	Coef (SE)	Coef. (SE)	Coef (SE)
Economy (considerations)	0.129 (0.159)	0.165 (0.116)	-0.090 (0.129)	-0.186 (0.219)
Economy 2 (considerations)	0.149 (0.126)	0.254** (0.100)	0.560* (0.128)	0.188 (0.123)
Social 1 (considerations)	0.103 (0.172)	0.044 (0.102)	-0.121 (0.154)	0.173 (0.164)
Social 2 (considerations)	0.286** (0.123)	0.086 (0.087)	0.433** (0.176)	0.117 (0.125)
Security Risk (consideration)	-0.027 (0.056)	-0.002 (0.034)	-0.038 (0.033)	-0.092* (0.053)
Feelings Legal	0.026 (0.053)	-0.004 (0.042)	0.024 (0.042)	-0.113* (0.058)
Feelings Illegal	0.059 (0.065)	0.001 (0.039)	0.073* (0.037)	0.155** (0.058)
Latino	-0.241 (0.382)	-0.017 (0.256)	0.222 (0.235)	0.585* (0.341)
Asian	-0.092 (0.300)	-0.089 (0.227)	0.115 (0.203)	0.232 (0.322)
Black	0.493 (0.450)	0.198 (0.328)	0.012 (0.288)	0.442 (0.400)
Other	-0.122 (0.411)	-0.438 (0.343)	0.159 (0.298)	1.150 (0.513)
Relative/Friend	0.274 (0.274)	0.217 (0.162)	0.151 (0.164)	0.016 (0.231)
Constant	-0.392 (0.500)	-0.110 (0.404)	-2.828** (0.487)	-0.030 (0.548)
N	71	139	150	70
R Squared	0.346	0.167	0.395	0.418

*$p<0.10$ (two-tailed) ** $p<0.05$

immigrants, which reduce support, and feelings toward "illegal" immigrants, which increase support for progressive reforms. Across all three types of frames then, we again find that individuals who are exposed to a given frame give more weight to relevant considerations compared to their counterparts in the control group.

In sum, we find that frames play an important role in influencing the weight that citizens assign to different considerations when considering proposals for immigration reform. Being exposed to a certain type of frame causes individuals to weight considerations relevant to that frame even more heavily in their policy opinions. Thus, the content of the frames that receive more attention in the media can play an important role in what support for immigration reform ultimately looks like.

CONCLUSION

Many factors influence how Americans feel about immigrants and U.S. immigration policy. Our effort is to understand the effects of media frames in shaping attitudes toward immigration. While it is widely believed that the media play an important role in shaping immigration attitudes, surprisingly few studies empirically analyze whether this in fact is the case. Our study seeks to fill this gap.

As noted at the outset of this chapter, the civic discourse on immigration is one where consumers are exposed to multiple frames for and against immigration. Our effort here was to understand how these frames shape immigration attitudes. Using an experimental design, we tested the effects of economic, social/symbolic, and national security frames, which varied in tone, separately on policy attitudes. We then considered whether frames work by varying belief content and/or altering the weight given to existing considerations.

We found that the content of the frames, rather than the tone, mattered more with respect to influencing opinions on restrictive and punitive policies related to immigration. With respect to more progressive policy proposals, both the content and the tone of the frames worked in predictable ways. With respect to the mechanisms driving these effects, we find that they are driven more by the process in which frames alter the weight of existing considerations than by frames altering belief content.

The results have important implications for understanding how media frames or popular discourse on immigration may ultimately affect any reform outcomes. There is not a simple direct path of the content and tone of frames on immigration policy attitudes. More novel frames, such as those related to positive economic arguments and national security issues, may affect belief content and in turn policy attitudes. However, other frames, for which people have established evaluations, may not have any effect on belief content and individuals may react against them in reporting their overall policy opinions. That being said, the content of the frames certainly affected the weight given to different considerations (economic, social, security) on overall support for policy reform proposals. Therefore, the relative weight that the media give to different dimensions of immigration may have important effects on immigration policy opinions.

APPENDIX 3.1

TREATMENT ARTICLES

Article 1

"Immigration and Its Positive Effects on the Economy"

Microsoft executive, Bill Gates, leads small army of high-tech executives to Capitol Hill, urging lawmakers for more visas.

As recently as 10 years ago, only five states—New York, Texas, Florida, Illinois, and California—were dealing with serious immigration problems. Today, immigration affects all 50 states. According to recent estimates, there are an estimated 12 million undocumented workers living in the U.S.

There is widespread consensus that the system is broke and needs fixing. Several attempts at bipartisan reform have failed on the U.S. Senate floor. The Senate was divided between members seeking to give some legal status to 12 million undocumented workers and lawmakers who oppose such a move. The reform bill is tabled for now, since consensus could not be reached.

Business owners claim that increasing legal immigration is essential for global marketplace competition. The President's Council of Economic Advisors (CEA) concludes that foreign-born workers fuel economic output, create jobs, and increase earnings for native-born workers by as much as 80 billion a year.

Bill Gates of Microsoft led a small army of high-tech executives to Capitol Hill, urging lawmakers for more visas necessary to fill critical jobs. Undocumented workers also make up 20 percent of roofers, painters, butchers, groundskeepers, and cooks. One construction executive in Oregon said "It's hard work [construction]. The labor goes to the Hispanic worker who is hungry. Many Caucasian workers are just not willing to do the work."

The CEA found that U.S. born workers' real wages increased 3 to 5% due to working immigrants since they generally take jobs that complement U.S. workers. In the agricultural field, most immigrants work as agricultural laborers, while U.S. workers take jobs such as farm supervisors. Contrary to conventional wisdom, the CEA also finds that immigrants and their children have a "modest positive influence" on government spending, contributing more per person in tax dollars than they claim in government benefits and services.

Article 2

"Immigration and Its Harmful Effects on the Economy"

Critics argue that immigrants flood the U.S. job market with millions of workers who compete for low wage jobs and drive down wages and living standards.

As recently as 10 years ago, only five states—New York, Texas, Florida, Illinois, and California—were dealing with serious immigration problems. Today, immigration affects all 50 states. According to recent estimates, there are an estimated 12 million undocumented workers living in the U.S.

There is widespread consensus that the system is broke and needs fixing. Several attempts at bipartisan reform have failed on the U.S. Senate floor. The Senate was divided between members seeking to give some legal status to 12 million undocumented workers and lawmakers who oppose such a move. The reform bill is tabled for now, since consensus could not be reached.

Some argue that an increase in immigration would harm U.S. workers and burden state and local governments. Representative Byron L. Dorgan said an increase in the number of immigrants "floods the U.S. job market with millions of workers who compete at low wages, for jobs Americans are doing, 'driving' down American wages and living standards." Scholars estimate that illegal immigration pushed wages for unskilled labor down by as much as 8 percent in the last decade.

Undocumented workers also place a heavy financial burden on state and local governments, who are not reimbursed from the federal government. A nonpartisan think tank estimates that providing health care and education to an estimated 83,000 illegal immigrants in Oklahoma will cost the state $207 million annually.

Though state and local governments are not required to provide welfare and Medicaid services, social service workers are not compelled to check immigration status, thus illegal immigrants often receive benefits. Additionally, providing education to children of illegal immigrants costs the nation about 7.4 billion annually and as that number rises so will the costs to state and local governments.

Article 3

"Immigration Is a Part of Our Nation's History"

Immigrants contribute greatly to the economic and social advances of the U.S. historically.

As recently as 10 years ago, only five states—New York, Texas, Florida, Illinois, and California—were dealing with serious immigration problems. Today, immigration affects all 50 states. According to recent estimates, there are an estimated 12 million undocumented workers living in the U.S.

There is widespread consensus that the system is broke and needs fixing. Several attempts at bipartisan reform have failed on the U.S. Senate floor. The Senate was divided between members seeking to give some legal status to 12 million undocumented workers and lawmakers who oppose such a move. The reform bill is tabled for now, since consensus could not be reached.

Some argue that allowing for higher levels of immigration and providing a legal path to citizenship for undocumented workers in this country is necessary to uphold the foundation of our nation. America is, after all, a nation of immigrants.

Throughout history immigration has fostered cultural and economic vitality. When large-scale Irish, Italian, and Jewish immigration began, those new arrivals were disliked intensely in many of the eastern cities where they settled in large numbers. These immigrants contributed greatly to the economic and social advances of the U.S. historically. For example, a high proportion of U.S. Nobel laureates are children of immigrants.

According to Robert Putnam, a Harvard University professor, "immigrant integration happened not because 'they' became like 'us,' but because we learned to live with overlapping identities. We are comfortable with hyphens—Irish-Americans yesterday, Mexican-Americans tomorrow."

Today, immigrants are not only contributing to economic and cultural growth, but make up an increasing proportion of the U.S. military serving in Iraq. Soldiers such as Rafael Peralta, who saved five other marines in Fallujah, have demonstrated courage and sacrifice for a country they seek to be citizens of.

Article 4

"Are Immigrants the Cause of Social Volatility?"

There is a current political movement seeking to perpetuate a parallel culture that does not speak English and cannot fully participate in mainstream America.

As recently as 10 years ago, only five states—New York, Texas, Florida, Illinois, and California—were dealing with serious immigration problems. Today, immigration affects all 50 states. According to recent estimates, there are an estimated 12 million undocumented workers living in the U.S.

There is widespread consensus that the system is broke and needs fixing. Several attempts at bipartisan reform have failed on the U.S. Senate floor. The Senate was divided between members seeking to give some legal status to 12 million undocumented workers and lawmakers who oppose such a move. The reform bill is tabled for now, since consensus could not be reached.

Some argue that increasing immigration and granting amnesty to illegal immigrants threatens the fabric of U.S. society and causes the loss of our unique national identity. Members of Congress are concerned that today's immigrants are not assimilating into American culture.

One representative states, "previous generations of immigrants expected their children to learn English, only in the recent past have we seen a political movement seeking to perpetuate a parallel culture that does not speak English and cannot participate fully in mainstream America." A nonpartisan study shows schools failing in educating immigrant children, due to language barriers, resulting in these children becoming increasingly isolated from mainstream America.

Additionally, many immigrants lack the education necessary for success and given the high dropout rate among Mexican immigrants, the American dream appears unattainable. Poorly educated women are more likely to have children out of wedlock (half of immigrant children are born to unwed mothers), creating more social problems and welfare dependency. Finally, granting amnesty to illegal immigrants goes against America's foundation by rewarding lawbreakers and ignoring immigrants who played by the rules.

Article 5

"Immigration and Its Effects on National Security"

Failed border security was one of the reasons cited by the 9/11 commission for the events of that day.

As recently as 10 years ago, only five states—New York, Texas, Florida, Illinois, and California—were dealing with serious immigration problems. Today, immigration affects all 50 states. According to recent estimates, there are an estimated 12 million undocumented workers living in the U.S.

There is widespread consensus that the system is broke and needs fixing. Several attempts at bipartisan reform have failed on the U.S. Senate floor. The Senate was divided between members seeking to give some legal status to 12 million undocumented workers and lawmakers who oppose such a move. The reform bill is tabled for now, since consensus could not be reached.

Security officials argue that immigration reform must include increased border security. The U.S. Mexican border is nearly 2,000 miles long and is consistently used as an entry point for illegal drugs and criminal aliens. "The reality is that thousands of people from around the world are successfully sneaking into the United States," said David Stoddard, a border patrol veteran.

Since 9/11, agents from the U.S. Customs and Border Protection Agency have stopped 132 nationals from countries considered a national security threat, including Syria, North Korea, and Iran. Failed border security was one of the reasons cited by the 9/11 commission for the events of that day.

Security officials argue that immigration reform must include increased funding for hiring more personnel at the border, increased border fencing, increased vehicle barriers, and the installation of ground-based radar and camera towers along the southern border.

Border personnel alone should be increased to 10,000 full-time agents and border fencing increased by 700 miles throughout the Southwest. Others argue that a guest worker program greatly cuts down on the number of people trying to cross the border illegally, allowing agents to focus on those who pose a security threat.

APPENDIX 3.2

Policy Preference Measures

Congress has recently tried to overhaul our nation's immigration laws. On a scale from 0 to 10, how strongly do you support or oppose the following policies? A zero (0) means that you oppose strongly, a five (5) means you neither oppose nor support, and a ten (10) means you strongly support.

1. Build a 700 mile fence along the U.S.-Mexico border.
2. Increase spending on border security.
3. Hire 10,000 more personnel to secure our southern border.
4. Make all illegal immigrants felons and deport them to their country of origin.
5. Allow illegal immigrants to remain in the U.S. and become U.S. citizens, but only if they meet certain requirements like paying a fine and do not have a criminal record.
6. Create a guest worker program that allows immigrants to remain in the U.S. or come to the U.S. to work, but only for a limited amount of time.
7. Grant amnesty to all illegal immigrants, giving them lawful permanent residence and the chance to become U.S. citizens.
8. Increase the number of visas for skilled workers.

Considerations

We next have a series of questions pertaining to *legal immigration*. On a scale from 0 to 10, how strongly do you agree or disagree with the following statements? A zero (0) means that you disagree strongly, a five (5) means you neither agree nor disagree, and a ten (10) means you agree strongly.

1. There are too many immigrants in the U.S. today.
2. The nation's immigration system is working well.
3. Immigrants drive down the wages of U.S. workers.
4. Rather than take jobs away from Americans, immigrants take jobs Americans are not willing to do.
5. Immigrants and their children are a financial burden on state and local governments.
6. The growing number of newcomers from other countries threatens traditional American customs and values.
7. Throughout U.S. history, immigrants have contributed greatly to cultural, economic, and social advances.
8. Immigrants today are less willing to assimilate to the American way of life.
9. It is important to uphold the foundation of our nation as a nation of immigrants.

We next have a series of questions pertaining to *illegal immigration*. On a scale from 0 to 10, how strongly do you agree or disagree with the following statements? A zero (0) means that you disagree strongly, a five (5) means you neither agree nor disagree, and a ten (10) means you agree strongly.

1. Right now, it is easy for those who pose a security threat to enter the U.S. illegally by crossing the U.S.-Mexico border.
2. Illegal Immigrants come to the U.S. to work, not to do us harm.
3. Illegal immigrants drive down the wages of U.S. workers.
4. Illegal immigrants take jobs Americans don't want.
5. Illegal immigrants help the economy by providing low cost labor.
6. Illegal immigration has led to a growth in crime in America.
7. Illegal immigrants do not pose a burden to the social welfare system since they are not eligible for benefits.
8. Illegal immigrants do not even try to assimilate by learning English.

NOTES

1. Joseph Carroll, "Americans Divided on Need for New Immigration Laws," *Gallup*, July 16, 2007.

2. Daniel B. Wood, "Obama vs. Romney 101: 5 Ways They Differ on Immigration," *The Christian Science Monitor*, September 7, 2012.

3. Ted Brader, Nicholas A. Valentino, and Elizabeth Suhay, "What Triggers Public Opposition to Immigration? Anxiety, Group Cues, and Immigration Threat," *American Journal of Political Science* 52, no. 4 (2008): 959–78.

4. See, for example, Jack Citrin, Donald P. Green, Christopher Muste, and Cara Wong, "Public Opinion toward Immigration Reform: The Role of Economic Motivations," *Journal of Politics* 59, no. 3 (1997): 858–81.

5. On these various arguments, see Peter Brimelow, *Alien Nation: Common Sense about America's Immigration Disaster* (New York: Random House, 1995); Vernon M. Briggs Jr., *Mass Immigration and the National Interest* (New York: M. E. Sharpe, 1996); and Patrick J. Buchanan, *State of Emergency: The Third World Invasion and Conquest of America* (New York: St. Martin's Griffin, 2006).

6. Thomas J. Espenshade and Charles A. Calhoun, "An Analysis of Public Opinion toward Undocumented Immigration," *Population Research and Policy Review* 12, no. 3 (1993): 189–224; and Citrin, Green, Muste, and Wong, "Public Opinion."

7. Desmond King, *Making Americans* (Cambridge, MA: Harvard University Press, 2000); Victoria M. Esses, John F. Dovidio, Lynne M. Jackson, and Tamara L. Armstrong, "The Immigration Dilemma: The Role of Perceived Group Competition, Ethnic Prejudice and National Identity," *Journal of Social Issues* 57 (2001): 389–412; and Paul Sniderman, Louk Hagendoom, and Markus Prior, "Predispositional Factors and Situational Triggers: Exclusionary Reactions to Immigrant Minorities," *American Political Science Review* 98 (2004): 35–50.

8. Espenshade and Calhoun, "Analysis of Public Opinion."

9. Buchanan, *State of Emergency*.

10. See, for example, Brader, Valentino, and Suhay, "What Triggers Public Opposition to Immigration?"; and Espenshade and Calhoun, "Analysis of Public Opinion."

11. Citrin, Green, Muste, and Wong, "Public Opinion"; M. V. Hood and Irwin L. Morris, "Amigo o Enemigo? Context, Attitudes, and Anglo Public Opinion toward Immigration," *Social Science Quarterly* 78, no. 2 (1997): 309–23; and Espenshade and Calhoun, "Analysis of Public Opinion."

12. Rodney E. Hero and Caroline J. Tolbert, "A Racial/Ethnic Diversity Interpretation of Politics and Policy in the States of the U.S.," *American Journal of Political Science* 40, no. 3 (1996): 851–71; and M. V. Hood and Irwin L. Morris, "Brother, Can You Spare a Dime? Racial/Ethnic Context and the Anglo Vote on Proposition 187," *Social Science Quarterly* 81 (2000): 194–206.

13. Espenshade and Calhoun, "Analysis of Public Opinion"; Citrin, Green, Muste, and Wong, "Public Opinion"; and Adrian Pantoja, "Against the Tide? Core American Values and Attitudes toward U.S. Immigration Policy in the Mid-1990s," *Journal of Ethnic and Migration Studies* 32 (2006): 515–31.

14. Marilyn Hoskin and William Mishler, "Public Opinion toward New Migrants," *International Migration* 21, no. 4 (1983): 440–61; Hood and Morris, "Brother, Can You Spare a Dime?"; and Pantoja, "Against the Tide?"

15. Citrin, Green, Muste, and Wong, "Public Opinion"; and Espenshade and Calhoun, "Analysis of Public Opinion."

16. On Latino and Asian attitudes, see Rodolfo de La Garza, Louis DeSipio, F. Chris Garcia, John A. Garcia, and Angelo Falcon, *Latino Voices: Mexican, Puerto Rican and Cuban Perspectives on American Politics* (Boulder, CO: Westview, 1992); and Pei-te Lien, M. Margaret Conway, and Janelle Wong, *The Politics of Asian Americans: Diversity and Community* (New York: Taylor and Francis, 2007). On Africa American attitudes, see Pantoja, "Against the Tide?"; and Adrian Pantoja, "Friends or Foes? African American Attitudes toward the Political and Economic Consequences of Immigration," in *Black and Latino/a Politics: Issues in Political Development in the United States*, eds. William E. Nelson and Jessica Lavariega Monforti (Miami, FL: Barnhardt and Ashe, 2005), 177–87.

17. Exceptions include Brader, Valentino, and Suhay, "What Triggers Public Opposition to Immigration?"; Benjamin R. Knoll, David P. Redlawsk, and Howard B. Sanborn, "Framing Labels and Immigration Policy Attitudes in the Iowa Caucuses: 'Trying to Out-Tancredo Tancredo,'" *Political Behavior* 33, no. 3 (2011): 433–54; and Jennifer L. Merolla, S. Karthick Ramakrishnan, and Chris Haynes, "'Illegal,' 'Undocumented,' or 'Unauthorized': Equivalency Frames, Issue Frames, and Public Opinion on Immigration," *Perspectives on Politics* 11, no. 3 (2013): 789–807.

18. See, for example, John Zaller, *The Nature and Origins of Mass Opinion* (Cambridge: Cambridge University Press, 1992); and Chris Haynes, "Vying for Conservative Hearts and Minds: Changes in Media Frames on Immigration since 2000" (see chapter 4 in this collection).

19. Brader, Valentino, and Suhay, "What Triggers Public Opposition to Immigration?"

20. Knoll, Redlawsk, and Sanborn, "Framing Labels."

21. Merolla, Ramakrishnan, and Haynes, "'Illegal,' 'Undocumented,' or 'Unauthorized.'"

22. On the importance of media, see Shanto Iyengar and Donald R. Kinder, *News That Matters: Television and American Opinion* (Chicago: University of Chicago Press, 1987).

23. See, for example, James N. Druckman, "On the Limits of Framing Effects: Who Can Frame?" *Journal of Politics* 63, no. 4 (2001): 1041–66; James N. Druckman, "Political Preference Formation: Competition, Deliberation, and the (Ir)relevance of Framing Effects," *American Political Science Review* 98, no. 4 (2004): 671–86; James N. Druckman and Kjersten R. Nelson, "Framing and Deliberation: How Citizens' Conversations Limit Elite Influence," *American Journal of Political Science* 47, no. 4 (2003): 729–45; and Thomas E. Nelson, Rosalee A. Clawson, and Zoe M. Oxley, "Media Framing of a Civil Liberties Conflict and Its Effect on Tolerance," *American Political Science Review* 91, no. 3 (1997): 567–83.

24. Nelson, Clawson, and Oxley, "Media Framing," 568.

25. Nelson, Clawson, and Oxley, "Media Framing"; Druckman, "On the Limits of Framing Effects"; and Druckman, "Political Preference Formation."

26. Nelson, Clawson, and Oxley, "Media Framing."

27. Ibid.; Thomas E. Nelson, Zoe M. Oxley, and Rosalee A. Clawson, "Toward a Psychology of Framing Effects," *Political Behavior* 19, no. 3 (1997): 221–46; and Thomas E. Nelson and Zoe M. Oxley, "Issue Framing Effect on Belief Importance and Opinion," *Journal of Politics* 61, no. 4 (1999): 1040–67.

28. See, for example, Druckman, "On the Limits of Framing Effects"; Druckman and Nelson, "Framing and Deliberation"; Shanto Iyengar, *Is Anyone Responsible?* (Chicago: University of Chicago Press, 1991); Thomas E. Nelson and Donald R. Kinder, "Issue Framing and Group-Centrism in American Public Opinion," *Journal of Politics* 58, no. 4 (1996): 1055–78; Nelson, Clawson, and Oxley, "Media Framing"; and Nelson and Oxley, "Issue Framing Effect." However, more recent work has shown that framing effects disappear if people are given two elite frames (see Paul M. Sniderman and Sean M. Theriault, "The Dynamics of Political Argument and the Logic of Issue Framing," in *Studies in Public Opinion: Attitudes, Nonattitudes, Measurement Error and Change*, eds. William E. Saris and Paul M. Sniderman [Princeton, NJ: Princeton University Press, 2004], 133–64) or if individuals exposed to different frames have a group conversation (see Druckman and Nelson, "Framing and Deliberation").

29. Nelson and Oxley, "Issue Framing Effect"; and Druckman and Nelson, "Framing and Deliberation."

30. Jennifer L. Merolla, Adrian D. Pantoja, Ivy A. M. Cargile, and Juana Mora, "From Coverage to Action: The Immigration Debate and Its Effects on Participation," *Political Research Quarterly* 66 (2013): 322–35.

31. The rotated factor loadings are as follows: legal wages 0.803; legal financial burden 0.802; illegal wages 0.798; and illegal financial burden 0.586.

32. The rotated factor loadings are as follows: legal take jobs 0.866; illegal come to work 0.515; illegal take jobs 0.836; and illegal help economy 0.676.

33. The rotated factor loadings are as follows: legal assimilate 0.805; illegal assimilate 0.807; and illegal crime 0.723.

34. The rotated factor loadings are as follows: legal values 0.545; legal contribute 0.809; and legal foundation 0.841.

35. While the results are in line with expectations, it is a bit puzzling that those in the economic and social frame conditions similarly weight economic considerations, while those in the former weight social considerations even more. It could be that exposing individuals to one of these frames makes the other considerations accessible as well (the second process outlined in the theoretical section). That is, people may connect both the economic and social dimensions when they think about immigration.

36. It is a bit surprising that the coefficient on *Economy 2* is higher for those in the social frame column compared to the economic frame column. Again, it could be that the frame makes related considerations more accessible.

FOUR

Vying for Conservative Hearts and Minds

Changes in Media Frames on Immigration since 2000

Chris Haynes

In the "Back of the Book" segment tonight, when President Obama was
elected, he promised a comprehensive immigration reform bill, also
known to some people as amnesty during his first year of his administration. Well, he failed to get it done so far, and the Latino community
is not happy. This week many of their leaders had a meeting at the
White House. So now the president wants the lame-duck Congress to
pass the so-called DREAM Act, which would provide amnesty to certain illegal aliens who go to college for a few years or who serve in the
military. . . . How is that fair to the Latino kids who are here legally and
trying to get that in-state tuition?. . . What about the American people?
What about those people? What do you say to those families who feel
that their children are denied opportunities?
            —Laura Ingraham, *The O'Reilly Factor*, November 18, 2010

This excerpt from the cable news program *The O'Reilly Factor* illustrates
the complexity of the immigration policy discourse over the past decade.
Here, conservative radio personality Laura Ingraham mentioned at least
seven different policy frames to describe the DREAM Act.[1] Moreover, its
diversity, complexity, and nuance are more the rule than the exception in
terms of conservative coverage of immigration policies. This matters because we know that these different frames can tap into different emotions, bring to mind different considerations, prime different images, and
systematically affect immigration preferences.[2] Considerations are any-

69

thing that a person uses to construct or formulate an opinion. Following political communication conventions, images are representations that serve as a mental receptacle for related considerations. Priming is bringing to the fore specific representations that can systematically affect an individual's opinions.[3]

And even though previous research finds that the public's opinions on immigration are extremely complex and nuanced, most research on immigration still uses a simple and blunt measure of immigration support, namely, the extent to which Americans want to see an increase or decrease in immigration.[4] In the last two decades, however, political discourse on immigration has grown to include discussions on a number of different policies, including birthright citizenship (BC), the DREAM Act, and driver's licenses. Additionally, media accounts have begun to use a variety of different frames to describe immigrants themselves. However, scholarship is just beginning to investigate the relationship between the media and public opinion in these, more complicated policy terrains.

In this chapter, I address these gaps by presenting the findings of my media content analysis of immigration coverage in four of the most viewed cable news shows. Cable news shows have dominated the production of immigration policy news and opinion. Here, I provide a detailed account of news coverage of two immigration policies that have become prominent since 2000: BC and the DREAM Act. I explore the various frames that are invoked in the coverage of these two policies, and consider the ways in which they vary over time, across issues, and across news sources. In short, I find that conservative media coverage is indeed much more complex than the casual observer and seasoned researcher might expect. Coverage varies not only by policy but also over time and by cable program.

However, more than speaking to academia, I wish to engage with the broader public by exploring a question that is current and relevant. Specifically, I describe the contours of conservative media framing of immigration policies that few now doubt as having played one of the most consequential roles in the downfall of the comprehensive immigration reform (CIR) in 2006–2007. This keeps with the spirit of public sociology whose primary objective is to transcend the academy by engaging in research that defines, promotes, and informs public debate on contemporary issues.[5]

This research is even more important today now that the issue of immigration reform is again front and center thanks to the results of the 2012 election, the persistence of immigration activists, and the willingness of politicians to engage in a major push to finally address this issue in a comprehensive fashion. Understanding the nuances, particularities, and role of conservative talk media on the topic of undocumented immigration could inform current and future strategies by which immigration advocates can deflect and combat what is sure to be more nativist and racist sentiment in the upcoming CIR debate. In short, this research should not only provide needed information to advocates on the ground but also encourage political scientists to conduct research with an expressly practical objective (refer to table 4.1 for content analysis specifics).

FRAMING BIRTHRIGHT CITIZENSHIP

The question as to whether citizenship should be granted to anyone who is born on U.S. soil has spanned the last decade. Again, what might seem very simple to most is quite complex. In this section, I discuss the issue of BC; the different frames employed in its coverage; and their variations across time (last decade) and space (cable program). The data I present come from a content analysis of BC on four major cable programs (*The O'Reilly Factor, Hannity & Colmes, Glenn Beck*, and *Lou Dobbs Tonight*) since 2000.[6] Here, I analyze cable segments on immigration and BC from the same cable programs since 2000.[7] I examine variance in the coverage of BC during and after important events, including the Saul and Elvira Arellano deportation story (2006–2007) and the comments made by maverick Senator Lindsey Graham (R-SC) on the issue in 2010. Generally, BC coverage was less frequent than that of the DREAM Act.

The media's framing of BC has been complex and varied. Since 2000, fifteen different frames of the BC policy emerge. These frames include the following: *constitutionality, disease, criminality, fiscal drain, rule of law, backdoor amnesty, taking advantage, race card, racializing, encouraging more illegal immigration, rewarding bad behavior, unfairness to legal immigrants, political pandering, humanistic*, and *anti-baby* (see table 4.2 for more on these frames). While eleven frames were either restrictive or neutral, only four were permissive.

2000–2005: The Dead Period

The first few years of the twenty-first century were relatively uneventful in terms of BC coverage. Even early efforts by Rep. James Sensenbrenner (R-WI) to enact immigration reform failed to spark cable coverage. The three shows that were on the air (*The O'Reilly Factor, Lou Dobbs Tonight*, and *Hannity & Colmes*) only produced a total of eight segments on BC (*The O'Reilly Factor* = 3, *Hannity & Colmes* = 2, *Lou Dobbs Tonight* = 3).

Table 4.1. Content Analysis of Cable News Coverage, Key Aspects

Time Period	2000 to 2011	2000 to 2011	2003 to 2009	2006 to 2010
News Anchors	Bill O'Reilly	Sean Hannity	Lou Dobbs	Glenn Beck
Issues		Birthright DREAM	citizenship Act	

Table 4.2.   Birthright Citizenship Frames

Constitutionality	Changing the U.S. Constitution to eliminate BC policy
Disease	Undocumented spreading disease, threatening our security/safety
Criminality	Increasing crime, drug, or gang activity as a result of BC policy
Fiscal Drain	Undocumented use up public resources, cost taxpayers money
Rule of Law	These are lawbreakers, we must uphold the rule of law
Backdoor Amnesty	Backdoor or stealth amnesty, anchor baby to get relatives legal status
Taking Advantage	Undocumented taking advantage of our generosity, Constitution
Race Card	Immigrant supporters calling critics of BC policy racists for opposing it
Racializing	Associating immigrant racial/ethnic group with BC policy
Encouraging More Illegal Immigration	Chain migration, incentivizing more illegal immigration
Rewarding Bad Behavior	BC policy rewards those with citizenship who break the law
Unfairness to Legal Immigrants	Unfair to grant citizenship to undocumented ahead of those who are in line or legal immigrants who have waited in line
Political Pandering	Politicians who are pushing permissive policies to appease their supporters and get more votes
Humanistic	Empathetic stories about the human cost of keeping dreamers in the shadows
Anti-Baby	Opposing BC policy is picking on innocent babies and children who have no culpability

And while we should not draw any solid generalization from this data, we can analyze the content and framing of these segments to see if there were any differences in emphasis. I find differences in topical focus and frames usage.

First, I find that for the first time the fact that *Hannity & Colmes* is hosted by both Sean Hannity (conservative) and Alan Colmes (liberal) has an effect on the clarity in framing of the segment. In other words, even though Hannity usually dominates the conversation, the fact that liberal cohost Colmes does at times engage in the discussion muddles the program's message. I illustrate this in the next two excerpts taken from an interview with Rep. Gary Miller (R-CA). Hannity stated:

But first, under the current law, any child born on American soil is awarded U.S. citizenship. So if an illegal immigrant makes it safely across the border, any of her children born here enjoy all the benefits of citizenship. And those kids can even sponsor their parents for citizenship after they turn 21. But a new bill before Congress would deny automatic citizenship to the children of illegal immigrants. [8]

However, the conversation quickly turned from these negative frames into a discussion of the meaning of the Fourteenth Amendment about the *constitutionality* of the bill.

COLMES: Well, the 14th Amendment is one of the bedrocks of our law, and conservatives usually get after the Supreme Court when they talk about looking at other countries and what they do. The San Diego Union says that since the people impacted are already citizens under the current law, what your legislation does would really revoke one citizenship, which is something usually reserved for traitors. You'd be taking citizenship away from somebody born in this country.

MILLER: We're not taking away, we just don't think we should grant it. This is subject to the jurisdiction thereof. You can't tell me that a woman in this country having a child here is subject to the jurisdiction of the United States. They're not. They're subject to jurisdiction of.

COLMES: That's not what the 14th Amendment says. I mean, granted it was—that amendment came forth in 1868, but it doesn't specify slavery in the amendment, and you would then have to change the Constitution. This would not withstand a legal test.

MILLER: Would not have to change the Constitution. [9]

One commonality in Hannity's coverage is the mention of the rule of law, which for BC is part of the *constitutionality* frame. Again I emphasize the effect of having an ideological diversity.

Another point of distinction is that Bill O'Reilly's segments employed different policy frames than the other anchors. His first story in particular is quite striking in its claim that BC is attracting "disease-ridden illegals" to the United States. O'Reilly is the only host to make this claim as it pertains to BC. The following illustrates this *disease* frame: "You know what's going to tilt this? The communicable diseases we're going to talk about in a minute. That's the only thing that's going to get the attention of the mainstream American, if illegal people start to bring in these diseases, all right." [10] Moreover, O'Reilly was the only host to frame the BC issue in *criminality* terms.

Finally, Lou Dobbs placed greater emphasis on the *encouraging more illegal immigration* frame than the other hosts. In total, Dobbs aired two segments that placed the chain migration argument front and center. For example: "Every year, almost 300,000 babies are born to illegal aliens in this country. Those babies are called anchor babies because every one of them instantly becomes a U.S. citizen, anchoring them to the United States. And with that privilege comes access to this country's public benefits and the right to petition the government to make the rest of their family legal citizens."[11] Although Hannity did mention the *encouraging more illegal immigration* frame once, the majority of this conversation dealt with the constitutional question raised by his liberal cohost Colmes.

In summary, in terms of the ideological clarity of the policy framing, segments by Hannity and Colmes were less clear than by Dobbs and O'Reilly. In terms of policy frames, O'Reilly was the only anchor to emphasize the *disease* and the *criminality* frames in his portrayal of BC. While these differences may be somewhat overstated, they still describe a varied media presentation of the BC policy.

The Saul and Elvira Arellano Deportation (2006–2007)

In 2006, these cable shows covered the case of a mother and son who were the subject of a national debate on deportation. Elvira Arellano was an undocumented immigrant who came to America in 1997. While living in Illinois, Elvira had a son, Saul. Since he was born in the United States, he was a U.S. citizen. However, in 2002, Elvira was caught up in a security sweep of Chicago's O'Hare Airport; she was arrested and ordered to surrender to authorities for deportation. She failed to show up for her deportation. To evade authorities, she took refuge in the Adalberto Methodist Church in Chicago where she remained under church protection for over a year. She was finally apprehended in Los Angeles on August 19, 2007, and was subsequently deported in 2008. Elvira's story became the subject of a nationwide debate on deportation, separation of children from their mothers, and BC.

Did this event affect the level of cable coverage of BC? Additionally, did the nature of the coverage vary by conservative media outlet? In terms of volume of coverage, there is no doubt that the Arellano case motivated coverage on the BC issue on *Lou Dobbs Tonight*. During the salient period (August 2006 to August 2007), Dobbs produced six segments on BC. By contrast, *Glenn Beck* only aired two segments, while *Hannity & Colmes* and *The O'Reilly Factor* only ran one each. Moreover, while five of the six segments on Dobbs's show explicitly talked about Arellano, this is the case only for one story on *Glenn Beck* and no stories for the other two shows. Dobbs's coverage was simply more focused on the controversy.

Furthermore, Dobbs employed more frames in his coverage of the case. By presenting coverage that focused on Arellano, Dobbs implicitly promoted the *humanistic* frame alongside his more restrictive *rule of law, fiscal drain,* and *rewarding bad behavior* frames. He allowed the issue to take on very humanistic themes. In one segment, Saul, the young son, stated: "I'm going to tell them to tell President Bush to stop the deportation of my mom." On the same segment, Casey Wian, a Cable News Network (CNN) news correspondent, maintained:

While speaking to Mexican lawmakers, [he] won a new supporter back in the United States. New Mexico governor Bill Richardson wrote to President Bush pleading for leniency in the case. His letter reads, "Seven-year-old American citizen Saul Arellano is currently leading an international effort to save his mother from deportation." But the campaign is really being led by activists who support amnesty for all illegal aliens. Richardson goes on to state their case, writing, "The Arellano case puts a spotlight on the danger of not acting on a comprehensive immigration plan. Inaction puts our most vulnerable citizens, the estimated three million American citizen children of illegal immigrants, at risk." [12]

In contrast, O'Reilly emphasized the *fiscal drain* and *constitutionality* frames, Beck used the *fiscal drain, rule of law*, and *humanistic* frames, and Hannity employed the *rewarding bad behavior* and *unfairness to legal immigrants* frames. Thus, while it is unclear if there are significant differences in the policy framing between media programs, it is still true that the coverage in general involved the use of a wide variety of policy frames. Thus, combined with the differences in volume of coverage, this time period still lends support to the case that conservative coverage of BC was complex.

Maverick Senator Lindsey Graham (R-SC) Speaks (2010)

In July 2010, Senator Graham surprised many political observers by calling for hearings to rethink BC policy. While Graham had previously been a strong advocate for CIR, and was considered one of the last remaining Republican moderates on immigration after John McCain took on a more restrictive position in 2008, he too seemed to be tacking to the right. Explaining his support for exploring a constitutional amendment to change citizenship policy, Graham noted in 2010: "Half the children born in hospitals on our borders are the children of 'illegal immigrants.' It will stop if we change the law that gives them citizenship by birth." [13] This single mention resurrected the BC issue, which had all but disappeared after the Arellano deportation in 2007.

Did these statements have any effect on cable coverage of BC? Yes and no. First, in terms of coverage volume, Graham's change in position generated more coverage only on *The O'Reilly Factor*. I count four segments that were aired on *The O'Reilly Factor* on the issue of BC in the time period immediately following Graham's comments. To be clear, Dobbs's show had already ended on CNN by the time Graham made these comments. Thus, I only compare O'Reilly to Hannity and Beck. *Hannity & Colmes* aired only two small segments on how Senate Majority Leader Harry Reid (D-NV) once opposed BC, while *Glenn Beck* ignored the issue altogether. Second, despite the higher volume of coverage on the *The O'Reilly Factor*, few differences if any emerged across the three cable programs.

Almost all segments discussed the *constitutionality* frame. In short, evidence from the period surrounding Graham's comments suggest that the few differences in volume and framing that emerge from the transcripts are less to do with his remarks and more attributable to idiosyncrasies by program or host. In sum, although differences in framing and coverage do abound during this period, the dearth of coverage of the BC policy makes it difficult to confirm my claims.

A Comparative Look at BC Coverage by Program

In addition to the complexity demonstrated by the sheer number and diversity of frames that characterize the BC debate, an analysis of their use by the different hosts can reinforce this theme. Thus, I turn to the analysis of coverage by sources. In short, there is tremendous variation among cable programs in terms of the choice of immigration policies covered. Additionally, I find differences in the salience and choice of policy frames employed by the different cable outlets.

First, in terms of the frequency of coverage, *Lou Dobbs Tonight* devoted the most airtime to the BC issue (fourteen segments). His coverage was especially high in 2005 and 2006. *The O'Reilly Factor* was second (nine segments), followed by *Hannity & Colmes* and *Glenn Beck* (six segments each). Again, Beck's lower volume is partly a function of his short stint as a television host, starting at *CNN Headline News* in 2006, and moving to *Fox News* in 2009. Most striking is the fact that even though Dobbs left CNN in November 2009, his coverage is still the most prolific of all four cable shows.

Second, there are distinct differences in their argumentation styles. In short, O'Reilly and Hannity tended to use a more rational, abstract, and less personal style. In contrast, Beck and Dobbs tended to be more personal and emotional, and often described children as inanimate objects. By the time Dobbs began reporting on this issue in 2005, his coverage had already transformed into much more of an opinion show, with a decidedly incendiary and restrictive point of view. Unsurprisingly, his coverage was the most personal, emotion-laden, and striking for the way it objectified babies. For example: "Up next, this anchor baby paraded around in an attempt to keep the U.S. government from deporting *its* illegal alien mother. She's hiding—well, she's not really hiding, she's taken refuge in a Chicago Methodist church."[14] Beck used similar language in his segments as illustrated in the following excerpt:

> Oh, you're exactly right. Families shouldn't be separated. Gee, I wonder who made that decision? We didn't allow you to live here, Elvira. You snuck in and broke the law. The one thing you were just referring to that was broken. You finally got what you deserved. . . . The only one responsible for Elvira's plight is Elvira. She chose to sneak into

America two times. She chose to use a fake Social Security card. She chose to have her child here in America.[15]

This coverage stands in stark contrast to O'Reilly's. As the next excerpt illustrates, O'Reilly's BC coverage was more cerebral and witty as well as less personal and emotional.

Then there are the anchor babies born to illegal aliens on American soil. Under the 14th Amendment they automatically become citizens. Think about it. Do you think the country wanted that when it ratified the 14th Amendment in 1868? Of course not. That amendment was designed to make sure that free slaves got citizenship. Now it's used to encourage foreigners to sneak across our borders to give birth. Thus the Constitution is being misused.[16]

Although O'Reilly used some of the same terms as Beck and Dobbs, he actually constructed a more historical, legal, and broadly framed argument about the intent of the Fourteenth Amendment and connected it to contemporary implications. Conversely, Beck personalized his argument in a concrete story about Elvira. In the following excerpt, Hannity attempted to use reason to convince his guest that changing the law is reasonable.

Here is the difference, though, between your position and mine. If you don't respect our law, if you don't respect our country's sovereignty, if you don't have enough respect for this country, then I think this law needs to be rescinded about children becoming citizens. And you've got to—you can't cut in front of the line. Do you know what it's like? It's like if we're in line for the movies and then some other people cut in front? Is that fair? It's not. There are people that wait seven, eight years to get legal entry into this country, and other people don't respect it. And then they come, and then they can win a prize even though they weren't here legally. That bothers a lot of people. You've got to understand that.[17]

Finally, though there are some commonalities in policy framing of BC across all shows, there is also significant variation. The most common frame that each show dealt with is the *constitutionality* frame. Each show spent a substantial amount of airtime discussing the Fourteenth Amendment's wording and meaning, the intent of Congress when it was written, and the implications for today's application of BC. Additionally, I find frequent use of the *fiscal drain* frame in all shows. For example, Ingraham noted on *The O'Reilly Factor*:

The 2004 GAO [Government Accountability Office] Report, which I know you're familiar with, two or three states ended up being able to get the figures together of how much it costs to educate illegal aliens in the United States. 50 million to 87 million in Pennsylvania. Check this figure out for Texas. 932 million to $1 billion for the state of Texas. Are you saying, Francisco, tonight, that there is no reason taxpayers in

Texas whether they're Latino or whether they're American, whatever, that they shouldn't be outraged that they're footing the bill for illegal alien education and also health care? [18]

Yet a number of interesting differences emerge as well. First, while each show employed about the same number of different frames, differences emerge in terms of the number of frames that they employed per segment. Interestingly, Beck used the fewest number of frames per segment (1.67) of all the hosts. This indicates quantitatively what I noticed qualitatively that his presentation was usually very simple and unidimensional. By contrast, Hannity employed an average of about 2.87 frames per segment on the BC issue, with O'Reilly at 2.0 and Dobbs in between at 1.9 frames per segment.

Additional variation emerged within the *rule of law* frame that each host employed quite frequently throughout. Remarkable was the finding that Dobbs was the only host who concentrated more on explaining the definition and meaning of the Fourteenth Amendment than on discussing changing the Constitution. For much of his coverage, Dobbs was not satisfied that the amendment actually applied to "illegal immigrants." Therefore, his coverage focused on exploring the definition, meaning, and implications of the amendment to current "illegal immigrants" and citizenship questions. Consequently, Dobbs did not move on to discussions of the *constitutionality* frame until well after the other cable anchors. In the following excerpts from 2006, we see that in Dobbs we have a host who had not accepted the fact that illegal immigrant babies are guaranteed U.S. citizenship under the Fourteenth Amendment.

Members of the Texas legislature tonight are preparing to take aim at the legal interpretation of the 14th Amendment, the amendment that grants automatic citizenship under that interpretation to any child born in the United States—so-called "anchor babies." And America's most well-known anchor baby has returned to the United States from his trip to Mexico. In Mexico, he was used by open border advocates to persuade Mexican lawmakers to intervene in the United States. Jonathan Freed reports tonight on the return of Saul Arellano to his mother in Chicago, who remains holed up in a church fighting deportation. [19]

In contrast, as much as he abhorred the fact that illegal immigrant babies are guaranteed U.S. citizenship, Beck accepted it and moved on to the question of changing it.

Now, 140 years after the amendment was ratified, it has nothing to do with the children of slaves anymore. Now it's all about the children of illegal immigrants. . . . Now, over the years, there has been a ton of attempts to change the 14th Amendment, but they've all failed because—I mean, let's play the P.C. [politically correct] cards face up—no politician wants to be seen as hating newborns or, quite honestly, to be called a racist for helping repeal something that is so strongly associated with helping African-Africans. But now another bill is under consideration in the House, and it has been gathering quite a bit of support.[20]

Another point of distinction in the overall coverage is that *The O'Reilly Factor* was the only show to include discussions of the *criminality* frame. This example shows how guest host Heather MacDonald (from the Manhattan Institute) framed BC in criminal terms:

> What we are seeing as well is second and third generation Hispanics who, by definition, are American citizens, because of our birthright citizenship law here, they are joining gangs at increasing rates. I've had reports from Chicago that recruitment starts as early as nine-years-old. You talk to people in Washington, D.C., they say for every kid we can get out of a gang, two or three more take their place. And again, this is not just a phenomenon of illegal aliens.[21]

In contrast, other anchors and their guests did not tread on this topic.

In summary, comparisons by cable show reveal a significant amount of inter-show variation for BC. Differences emerge in terms of frequency, argumentation style, complexity in terms of number of frames used, and issue framing. And although there were some similarities in policy framing, coverage was far from uniform.

FRAMING THE DREAM ACT

Debates over DREAM Act proposals to create a pathway to citizenship for undocumented immigrant children living in the United States have spanned a decade since the original bill was introduced by Senators Orrin Hatch (R-UT) and Edward Kennedy (D-MA) in 2002. It would grant citizenship to undocumented children who came to the United States before the age of sixteen who stay out of trouble and go to college or serve in the military. Other versions of this legislation primarily on the state level offer tuition scholarships and other benefits to these same children. An issue that may seem simply about giving children the ability to acquire citizenship is in reality much more complex. In this section, drawing from my content analysis of the DREAM Act on the same four conservative cable shows since 2000, I discuss the media's framing and coverage of the act and how they varied across time and cable networks.[22]

Conservative media's framing of the DREAM Act has been complex and varied. Since 2000, at least fourteen different frames emerge, including *rewarding bad behavior, they're not like "us," fiscal drain, unfairness to legal immigrants, backdoor amnesty, national security, political pandering, encouraging more migration, rule of law, racializing, government incompetence, undocumented pay taxes too, pragmatism,* and *humanistic* (see table 4.3 for more on these frames). Most of these frames were negative in tone and restrictive in content (ten of thirteen).

There were three major periods during which the political calculus and process surrounding the DREAM Act changed in significant ways: the introduction of the DREAM Act (2001–2002), efforts at CIR (2005–2007), and the 2008 presidential campaign and beyond (2008–2011). In short, I have found that there are interesting differences by show in terms of the amount of coverage devoted to the DREAM Act surrounding those significant events.

The Dream Act: The Initial Offering (2001–2002)

The recent salience and interest in the DREAM Act may obscure the fact that this piece of legislation was first introduced more than a decade

Table 4.3. DREAM Act Frames

Rewarding Bad Behavior	DREAM Act rewards those with citizenship who break the law
They're not like "us"	Undocumented as unassimilable, not speaking English, different
Fiscal Drain	Undocumented use up public resources, cost taxpayers money
Unfairness to legal immigrants	Unfair to grant citizenship to undocumented ahead of those who are in line or legal immigrants who have waited in line
Backdoor Amnesty	Backdoor or stealth amnesty, anchor baby to get relatives legal status
National Security	DREAM Act will let terrorists in and threaten national security
Political Pandering	Politicians who are pushing permissive policies to appease their supporters and get more votes
Encouraging More Migration	Chain migration, incentivizing more illegal immigration
Rule of Law	These are lawbreakers, we must uphold the rule of law
Racializing	Associating immigrant racial/ethnic group with DREAM Act policy
Government Incompetence	Government being unresponsive to the public, tin ear
Undocumented Pay Taxes Too	Undocumented pay taxes, society benefits from undocumented
Pragmatism	Let's be realistic and smart, they are already here and we can't just kick them out; getting rid of them would have disastrous economic consequences
Humanistic	Empathetic stories about the human cost of keeping dreamers in the shadows

ago, first by Rep. Chris Cannon (R-UT) on May 21, 2001, in the House, and later by Senator Hatch on August, 1, 2001, in the U.S. Senate. Surprisingly, in lieu of the current partisan divide over immigration policy, it was two Republicans who offered this proposal to create a path to citizenship for millions of children brought to the United States illegally by their parents before they were sixteen. Among other provisions, both proposals would rescind current federal laws that prohibited these undocumented children from receiving higher education benefits based on state residence unless a U.S. national.[23] These two bills received scant attention by the press at the time, primarily because they were introduced around the same time that Senators Kennedy and Sam Brownback (R-KS) and the George W. Bush White House were all seeking a more comprehensive approach to the problem of illegal immigration.

In short, all three conservative commentators, Dobbs, O'Reilly, and Hannity (Beck's show did not start airing until much later, in 2006), were either late to the game or did not attend to early DREAM Act coverage at all. One striking finding is that both Dobbs and Hannity did not run a single segment on the DREAM Act during this period. We can only assume that the issue flew beneath their radar or they did not find it newsworthy. O'Reilly was the only cable host to provide any coverage, only a single segment aired on July 31, 2002, a full fourteen months after Cannon introduced the bill in the House. In this excerpt, O'Reilly framed the issue as *rewarding bad behavior, encouraging more migration, fiscal drain,* and *unfairness to legal immigrants*:

> The first hole is that it encourages other people to come here with kids because they see if they can evade authorities for five years, they can get legal status. And the second thing is while it does save the taxpayer in the long run, welfare costs and things like that for people who don't have an education, in the short run, it means more government spending, my money and your money, spent on people who shouldn't be here in the first place.[24]

On the same segment, Hatch responded to critiques of the bill and offered his perspective by countering with *humanistic* and *pragmatism* frames.

> Well, I think that we could do a better job on illegal immigration. But yes, you are wrong on the other side of that coin, because it's estimated that about 50 percent of these illegal children who are here through no fault of their own in almost every case that they drop out of school. So this act would give them the incentive to get their high school degree, because once they get their high school degree, then they would qualify for in-state tuition. And it's a proven fact that if a young kid goes through—gets their high school degree, goes to college and gets a college degree and works the rest of their lives, that it means about $100,000 to the taxpayers of America.[25]

However, instructive of his more measured and less combative tone, O'Reilly ended by repeating his agreement with both restrictive and permissive arguments.

> Right. We want to be compassionate, but we want to be fair to all people, the people who are legally trying to get in here, the people, Americans who are paying exorbitant taxes. And we see a solution to this, using the military to help the border patrol. We hope you guys consider it. But your bill is compassionate. It does make sense on one level, and we always appreciate it.[26]

We can safely say that the coverage on the DREAM Act was sporadic. Additionally, as for the segment that did air, it was relatively balanced in tone, especially in comparison to other DREAM Act segments from other time periods.

The Time for Immigration Reform (2005–2007)

Soon after the 2004 election, the Bush administration made CIR a priority, encouraging efforts at bipartisan legislation. This sparked open rebellion within the Republican Party, as restrictionists, such as Rep. Tom Tancredo (R-CO) and Sensenbrenner, sought to derail CIR, pushing for restrictive measures that would make undocumented status and aiding illegal immigrants a felony offense. During this time, the DREAM Act received little news attention compared to HR 4437 (Border Protection, Antiterrorism and Illegal Immigration Control Act of 2005), pro-immigration rallies, and the 2006–2007 attempts at CIR. However, its coverage picked up during the latter part of 2007 as supporters offered it as a standalone proposal.

Still, there were differences in the frequency of cable news coverage of the DREAM Act during this period: scant for both Hannity (one segment) and O'Reilly (one segment), but frequent for Dobbs (twenty-three segments) and Beck (ten segments). From September to December 2007 alone, Dobbs and Beck ran fifteen and ten DREAM Act segments, respectively. In contrast, O'Reilly ran only one segment while Hannity aired none.

Second, there were also important variations in framing by anchor. For example, during this salient period in late 2007, the common thread for all shows was a focus on the *backdoor amnesty* frame. After 9/11, there were significant departures in terms of the use of secondary frames. In addition to being about the "impending amnesty," coverage on *Lou Dobbs Tonight* was described in terms of the *fiscal drain* frame. This is not surprising given the bad state of the U.S. economy at the time. Here is an example of Dobbs's fiscal focus:

> We really should support every child in—and really obviate any impact from the criminality or the illegality undertaken by their parents.

You're right. That really is the province of the United States. We should continue to add to the woes of the American workforce and add to the public welfare rolls and expense and continue to, really, to put on the public expense of what is for private profit, like illegal immigration.[27]

By contrast, Beck painted a more complex narrative of legislation being snuck in "the backdoor when nobody's looking" that will cause a horrible "amnesty" for these "illegal immigrants almost entirely from Mexico," in a drip, drip fashion, with "a few million from here, then a few million from over [t]here in some other act, and pretty soon, before you know it, we're eating the whole damn value meal without even knowing it."[28] For Beck, it was less about the fiscal impact than about the impending amnesty of the "Mexicans" (*racializing, backdoor amnesty*). Additionally, as explicit and incendiary as Dobbs can get, Beck certainly topped him in this period as exemplified by: "We, the people, said—I believe the phrase was 'No way, Jose.' And the legislation rightfully failed. But some in Congress are just like my 2-year-old son. Doesn't really like 'no.' You know, there is so much bull crap in the DREAM Act I don't even know where to start shoveling!"[29]

In contrast, the only time in which *The O'Reilly Factor* even mentioned the DREAM Act was on November 19, 2007, in which guest host Ingraham railed against a number of different immigration policies that failed to pass. In this opinion segment, Ingraham framed the DREAM Act and the other policies in *they're not like "us"* and *political pandering* terms.

My friends, this is lunacy. The English language unites us as a people. And it's a mainstay of the American culture. If assimilation was truly everybody's goal, then this would never have been an issue in the first place. . . . Six months ago, we heard what—we heard that illegal immigration was a problem for the GOP. But now after comprehensive reform, the Dream Act, and driver's licenses for illegals all went down in flames, it's now obvious that the issue is bad for Democrats. By bowing down to anti-English language radicals, Speaker [Nancy] Pelosi imperils her entire Democrat majority because next year, the voters will have their revenge.[30]

Even though the DREAM Act did come up, it is instructive that it was Ingraham who delivered it and not O'Reilly. Other than this segment, O'Reilly ignored the whole DREAM Act episode that both Beck and Dobbs seemed consumed by.

There are three striking variations I would like to highlight. Most notably are differences in frequency of coverage: high for Dobbs and Beck, low for Hannity and O'Reilly. Next, while the volume of coverage of the DREAM Act was relatively heavy for Dobbs and Beck, it was almost nonexistent for both O'Reilly and Hannity. This was particularly the case in the months prior to the 2007 Senate cloture votes. Finally, the frames invoked by the different hosts varied quite substantially. Dobbs was the only host to place significant emphasis on the *fiscal drain* frame. By contrast, Beck was much more interested in framing the DREAM Act as *political pandering* in *racializing* language. And while Ingraham did use a cultural reference similar to Beck's references to Mexicans, its appearance does not seem typical of O'Reilly himself given its isolated occurrence.

The Historic Election of 2008 and Beyond

In late 2007, the Democratic presidential primary process was in full swing with Senator Hillary Clinton (D-NY) as the frontrunner followed by Senators John Edwards (D-NC), Barack Obama (D-IL), and Joe Biden (D-DE). The presidential primary process interacted with the yearly debate over immigration reform more generally, and the DREAM Act specifically. For the first time, coverage of the DREAM Act by all four anchors was somewhat uniform in terms of volume. O'Reilly aired the most segments at six from the beginning of 2008 to the end of 2011. The other three anchors produced four segments each. In terms of timing, the majority of segments for each program aired in November and December 2010, when Senate Majority Leader Reid resurrected the DREAM Act during the lame duck session. During the session, Reid decided to attach it to the Defense Appropriations Bill in a last ditch effort to pass the DREAM Act after Democrats lost control of the House and six Senate seats. In terms of volume, Beck and Dobbs ran two segments each, while O'Reilly and Hannity produced four. It is interesting that *The O'Reilly Factor* became much more active (six segments) in discussing the DREAM Act after only running two spots in the previous ten years.

In terms of framing, there are differences by news program. First, similar to the prior period (2005–2007), the dominant frame for all anchors was the *backdoor amnesty* frame. Also in a similar vein, there was variation on secondary framing. For example, while Beck and O'Reilly raised the *national security* frame, Dobbs's and Hannity's coverage were devoid of such mentions. The following excerpt illustrates how Beck raised the issue of terror to talk about the DREAM Act.

> The Dream Act would set into motion a process for granting amnesty to 2.1 illegal immigrants plus their 1.4 million parents and siblings who would also be legalized. But there is another reason to be against illegal immigration—security. It is my main reason. Has anyone noticed that there are people in the world that want to kill us? Never forget the 9/11 hijackers. What happened there? They overstayed their visas. Illegal immigrants don't even have visas. . . . It also seems to be the case for the Jordanian teenager in Texas. This guy was accused of trying to make a weapon of mass destruction to blow up a skyscraper in Dallas.[31]

Unlike Beck and O'Reilly, Dobbs and Hannity did not bring up the national security argument. In this spot from the same year, Dobbs chose a variety of frames, including *rewarding bad behavior, unfairness to legal immigrants,* and *fiscal drain.* He stated: "New legislation tonight could provide amnesty for illegal alien students across the country. It's the so-called Dream Act. It would also provide lower tuition rates to those students even though many American students wouldn't be eligible for the same break." Reporter Lisa Sylvester continued on the same episode: "The Dream Act was introduced in previous Congresses, but always rejected. Critics blast it as outright amnesty, saying it rewards people who ignore the law. U.S. unemployment is at the highest level in 25 years and amnesty may be a tough sell says one vocal opponent." [32]

As in prior periods, Hannity used a simple DREAM Act framing strategy during Obama's first term. In addition to the *backdoor amnesty* frame, he also invoked the *political pandering* frame to argue that it was attached to the Defense Appropriations Bill just to win votes. This excerpt came on the heels of the Democrats losing the House and followed reports suggesting that Democrats would push the DREAM Act during the 2010 lame duck session. "Putting that aside. We just had an election. This Congress was thrown out. The American people do not want amnesty. If they ram this down America's throat during the lame duck session, you don't think there are political consequences for that?" [33]

Overall, due to the dearth of coverage from this period, I make some cautious inferences about cable news coverage of the DREAM Act. First, while the volume was similar across shows during these years, it is important to note that O'Reilly became much more active beginning in 2010 than he was in the previous decade. Second, although the primary frame of reference for all anchors was the *backdoor amnesty* frame, there were variations in the secondary frames that each employed. Whereas Beck and O'Reilly made it a point to bring up the *national security* frame, Dobbs and Hannity did not. Instead Hannity preferred to focus on invoking the *political pandering* frame while Dobbs relied on a mix of other frames. Thus, regarding the totality of DREAM Act coverage, I found strong evidence, both in comparing the coverage of different anchors and looking at their development over time, of significant variation, complexity, and nuance.

A Comparative Look at Coverage by Program

By reviewing the different ways in which the anchors framed the DREAM Act over the past decade, we see the intricacy of this issue. I now turn to analysis of the coverage by sources. In short, differences between programs exist in terms of the choice of immigration policies covered. Additionally, I find differences in the salience and choice of policy framing employed by the different cable outlets. In this section, I present my

findings on frequency, national or local level focus, anchor argumentation style, and policy framing.

First, in terms of the frequency of coverage, Dobbs produced the most
segments on the DREAM Act (thirty segments). This finding is consistent
with the evidence from analysis of BC. However, in slight contrast to BC,
Beck ran the second most segments on the DREAM Act (fourteen segments). By no means is fourteen segments definitive evidence that Beck
was obsessed with the DREAM Act, but it does suggest that he was
certainly more interested in it than in BC (zero segments). O'Reilly was
third at eight segments with Hannity last with only six segments. Most
striking is the fact that even though Dobbs's and Beck's stints were the
shortest of the four anchors (Dobbs 2000–2009, Beck 2006–2011, and
O'Reilly and Hannity 2000–2011), they produced the most segments on
the issue of the DREAM Act.

Second, my findings on the argumentation styles of the different anchors in discussing the DREAM Act are consistent with that of BC. In
short, O'Reilly and Hannity tended to use a more rational, fact-finding,
abstract, and less personal argumentation style. Conversely, Beck's and
Dobbs's segments tended to be personal and emotional, and they bor-
dered on racist/classist. By the time Dobbs began reporting on this issue
(late 2004) his coverage had already become more opinionated, with a
decidedly restrictive point of view. However, in terms of argumentation
style, it is a toss-up as to whether his or Beck's coverage was the most
emotion laden and personal. This excerpt presents typical coverage by
Dobbs:

> Speaking of disgusting, Majority Leader Harry Reid, he's still all excit-
> ed about that amnesty agenda for illegal aliens. This so-called senator is
> promising to bring the DREAM Act to a vote before Nov. 16. Now, the
> DREAM Act, of course, would give U.S. citizenship to thousands of
> illegal alien students in this country. . . . Now these geniuses get to take
> another run at it.[34]

This next excerpt shows how Beck often used *racializing* language: "But
here is where it gets good. If he does absolutely nothing, California's
DREAM Act will become law. And illegal immigrants, *almost entirely from
Mexico*, but *I don't care where they're from*. We'll be rewarded with a cheaper education than your kids. That, by the way, is against the law. And
they'll also get green cards for the whole family."[35] This coverage stands
in stark contrast to that of O'Reilly and Hannity. As shown by the following statement, O'Reilly's coverage contained more discussion of rational
arguments and was less personal.

> A new bill called the Dream Act would ensure that young illegals who
> have spent five years in the USA would become legal residents after
> high school graduation. And the bill would also subsidize tuition for
> illegal aliens at some colleges. Joining us now from Washington is Re-

publican Senator Orrin Hatch of Utah, who sponsored the Dream Act. Now, I understand the compassionate nature of this, and the practical nature of the act as well. But, you know, there comes a point, Senator, where illegal activity is being rewarded, and you guys in Washington fail to confront the problem of illegal immigration. Am I wrong?

O'Reilly then continued with his more reason-giving argumentation style in the next passage in which he cited two different arguments supporting his opposition to the DREAM Act.

The first hole is that it encourages other people to come here with kids because they see if they can evade authorities for five years, they can get legal status. And the second thing is while it does save the taxpayer in the long run, welfare costs and things like that for people who don't have an education, in the short run, it means more government spending, my money and your money, spent on people who shouldn't be here in the first place.[36]

Finally, though there are some commonalities in framing of the DREAM Act that run throughout coverage on all shows, there are more differences. The most common frame that each anchor employed is *backdoor amnesty*. Each show dedicated a significant amount of airtime discussing how granting a pathway to citizenship to undocumented children equates to a *backdoor amnesty*. The following excerpt, by Beck, is a typical example of this oft-used frame: "It's like the—it's like the amnesty act. OK, we didn't get the amnesty, but they'll do the DREAM Act. Then they'll put this one in. Then they'll put this one in. These people will not give up. It's going to be relentless."[37]

Despite the similarities in the use of the *backdoor amnesty* frame across these shows, some striking differences emerge. While each show used the *backdoor amnesty* frame frequently, it accounts for different proportions of each anchor's overall framing. Dobbs's and Hannity's *backdoor amnesty* framing accounts for about 40 percent and 67 percent of their total frames, respectively. By contrast, for O'Reilly and Beck, the *backdoor amnesty* frame makes up only 20 percent and 25 percent of their total frames.

Another striking difference appears when we examine the total number of frames that each anchor used throughout their decade-long coverage of the DREAM Act. For example, while the three other anchors employed at least nine frames throughout their coverage of the act, Hannity only used three. This presents a stark contrast to the coverage on BC, where there was little to no variation in terms of the total number of different frames each anchor employed. This means that Hannity's coverage was framed in much narrower terms, usually using the *backdoor amnesty* frame. Consistent with this story, Hannity's coverage invoked the fewest frames per segment (1.5 frames/segment). By contrast, Dobbs used 1.6, O'Reilly 1.9, and Beck 2.2 frames/segment. This demonstrates quantitatively what I learned qualitatively: that Hannity's presentation of the

DREAM Act was usually simple and linear. Again this is interesting since it differs from my finding for BC coverage in which Hannity's and Beck's framing frequencies were reversed.

More variation emerged in use of the *political pandering* frame. Striking was the fact that while both Hannity and Beck used it frequently, this was not the case for Dobbs and O'Reilly. While the *political pandering* frame was the second most used frame for Beck and Hannity, it was tied for eighth and fifth for Dobbs and O'Reilly, respectively. Instead, Dobbs favored the *unfairness to legal immigrants* frame. Interestingly, as quoted earlier in this piece, Hannity instead opted for the *political pandering* frame. In contrast, Dobbs used the *unfairness to legal immigrants* frame. "The Senate bill incorporating the so-called Dream Act that gives in-state tuition to illegal aliens a benefit, of course, denied American citizens. Illegal aliens will, under the terms of this legislation, also be able to cut in front of everyone who have [*sic*] been waiting for years in their own countries for admission to the United States legally. Suckers."[38]

Another difference is that Dobbs was the only anchor to include a significant amount of discussion using the *fiscal drain* frame (seven segments). In contrast, O'Reilly used it once while Hannity did not use it at all. For example, Dobbs stated:

> But, you know what? We really should support every child in—and really obviate any impact from the criminality or the illegality undertaken by their parents. You're right. That really is the province of the United States. We should continue to add to the woes of the American workforce and add to the public welfare rolls and expense and continue to, really, to put on the public expense of what is for private profit, like illegal immigration.[39]

In sum, comparisons by cable shows reveal a significant inter-source variation for coverage of the DREAM Act. Differences appear in frequency of coverage, argumentation style, complexity in terms of number of frames used, and the way in which each host decided to frame this issue. Unlike the BC coverage, which was marked by a relatively high degree of commonality in media framing, DREAM Act coverage was more dissimilar.

CONCLUSION AND IMPLICATIONS

Here, I present a detailed analysis of the nature and tenor of conservative cable media's coverage of two different immigration policy issues: BC and the Dream Act. In short, the evidence strongly indicates that within conservative cable media, there is significant variation in coverage of undocumented immigration. I illustrate this variation between different policies and between cable shows. Between policies, coverage of BC was much less frequent than that of the DREAM Act. Within policies, certain hosts (Dobbs) seemed much more interested in the DREAM Act while others (O'Reilly) fancied BC. Additionally, argumentation style varied by host with some favoring a more reason-giving approach (O'Reilly) while others preferring entertaining and emotion-packed shouting matches (Dobbs, Beck). Moreover, there is also tremendous variation in policy framing. All told, there is significant nuance and complexity not only within the immigration policy debate (by policy), but also within the conservative media sphere (by program).

These findings have some important implications for how future research into the politics of undocumented immigration should proceed, and for how advocacy and public relations efforts on immigration reform should strategically unfold. First, given this complexity, we might expect to find systematic differences in public opinion across different policies. For instance, because of the dearth in coverage of BC in comparison to the DREAM Act, we might expect to find that preferences regarding BC to be more elastic and less resistant to persuasion. If these differences exist, it may be easier to change preferences on some policies and not others. Perhaps, immigration advocates should focus their messages on persuading preferences on less salient policies (e.g., DREAM Act).

Second, for much of the decade, conservative media were able to clearly articulate and dominantly establish multiple negative policy frames without a significant, resonant counter-frame. Additionally, other research I do in collaboration with other scholars finds that specific policy frames, such as *backdoor amnesty*, can have significant, negative effects on public support for a variety of immigration policies.[40] Together these findings suggest that much of the souring of public opinion and of the Congress that followed can be attributed to this establishment of this negative immigration frame. Moving forward, this suggests that if the new effort to enact CIR is to succeed, immigrant advocates in and out of government must do a more effective and consistent job of articulating and establishing their own frames. One such possibility is to leverage the power of empathy to gain entrée into the hearts and minds of the American public. I suggest this because in some related research, I find that empathetic frames can be effective drivers of permissive change in immigration preferences.[41] Regardless of the choice of frames, this public relations' strategy must be as comprehensive as the policy itself, spanning conservative, mainstream, and liberal media. Advocates cannot simply rely on rallying the faithful. For key House and Senate members to agree to support the bill, their undecided and conservative constituents *must* be among the persuaded.

Third, the complexity of the undocumented immigration discourse suggests that political science research should disaggregate current crude approaches to the study of immigration. No longer should studies analyze public support *just* for more or less immigration. Rather, we should employ separate models to explain each different policy preference.

Thus, in conclusion, I call for not only more research but also more poli-cy-specific research. This is how the next chapter on immigration opinion should be written.

NOTES

1. Policy frames are variations in terms used to discuss specific policy proposals that can bring to mind different arguments, associations, beliefs, stereotypes, and emotions.

2. On frames as they relate to immigration, see Ted Brader, Nicholas A. Valentino, and Elizabeth Suhay, "What Triggers Public Opposition to Immigration? Anxiety, Group Cues, and Immigration Threat," *American Journal of Political Science* 52, no. 4 (2008): 959–78; and Jennifer L. Merolla, S. Karthick Ramakrishnan, and Chris Haynes, "'Illegal,' 'Undocumented,' or 'Unauthorized': Equivalency Frames, Issue Frames, and Public Opinion on Immigration," *Perspectives on Politics* 11, no. 3 (2013): 789–807.

3. For further discussion on frames, see Shanto Iyengar and Donald R Kinder, *News That Matters: Television and American Opinion* (Chicago: University of Chicago Press, 1987); and James N. Druckman, Cari Lynn Hennessy, Kristi St. Charles, and Jonathan Webber, "Competing Rhetoric over Time: Frames versus Cues," *Journal of Politics* 72, no. 1 (2010): 136–48.

4. Marilyn Hoskin, *New Immigrants and Democratic Society: Minority Integration in Western Democracies* (New York: Praeger, 1991); Jack Citrin, Donald P. Green, Christopher Muste, and Cara Wong, "Public Opinion toward Immigration Reform: The Role of Economic Motivations," *Journal of Politics* 59, no. 3 (1997): 858–81; and Rita J. Simon, "Old Minorities, New Immigrants: Aspirations, Hopes, and Fears," *The Annals of the American Academy of Political and Social Science* 530 (1993): 61–73.

5. Michael Burawoy, "For Public Sociology," 2004 presidential address for the American Sociological Association, *American Sociological Review* 70 (2005): 4–28.

6. Programs were selected based on viewership. According to Nielsen, three of these shows were consistently in the top four between 2000 and 2011. The only exception is *Lou Dobbs Tonight*, which was the most watched non–Fox News Channel program.

7. Transcripts of the news programs were retrieved from LexisNexis using the following search terms: SHOW (*The O'Reilly Factor, Lou Dobbs Tonight, Glenn Beck,* OR *Hannity & Colmes*) AND illegal immigration OR illegal immigrants OR illegal aliens OR undocumented OR illegals AND birthright citizenship OR birthright OR anchor baby. Content analysis involved in-depth reading of each transcript retrieved.

8. Sean Hannity, *Hannity & Colmes*, July 12, 2005.

9. Alan Colmes and Gary Miller, *Hannity & Colmes*, July 12, 2005.

10. Bill O'Reilly, *The O'Reilly Factor*, April 23, 2003.

11. Lou Dobbs, *Lou Dobbs Tonight*, March 30, 2005.

12. Saul Arellano and Casey Wian, *Lou Dobbs Tonight*, November 17, 2007.

13. Lindsey Graham, *On the Record with Greta Van Susteran*, August 3, 2010.

14. Lou Dobbs, *Lou Dobbs Tonight*, December 4, 2006.

15. Glenn Beck, *Glenn Beck*, August 20, 2007.

16. Bill O'Reilly, *The O'Reilly Factor*, January 6, 2011.

17. Sean Hannity, *Hannity & Colmes*, January 9, 2007.

18. Laura Ingraham, *The O'Reilly Factor*, May 2, 2008.

19. Lou Dobbs, *Lou Dobbs Tonight*, November 20, 2006.

20. Glenn Beck, *Glenn Beck*, September 27, 2006.

21. Heather MacDonald, *The O'Reilly Factor*, August 17, 2004.

22. Transcripts of the news programs were retrieved from LexisNexis using the following search terms: SHOW (*The O'Reilly Factor, Lou Dobbs Tonight, Glenn Beck,* OR *Hannity & Colmes*) AND illegal immigration OR illegal immigrants OR illegal aliens

OR undocumented OR illegals AND DREAM Act OR DREAM. Content analysis involved in-depth reading of each transcript retrieved.

23. U.S. Congress, Senate Judiciary Committee, 107th Cong., 2d sess., http://thomas.loc.gov/cgi-bin/bdquery/z?d107:S1291:.

24. Bill O'Reilly, *The O'Reilly Factor*, July 31, 2002.

25. Orrin Hatch, *The O'Reilly Factor*, July 31, 2002.

26. Bill O'Reilly, *The O'Reilly Factor*, July 31, 2002.

27. Lou Dobbs, *Lou Dobbs Tonight*, October 27, 2007.

28. Glenn Beck montage, *Glenn Beck*, September 2007.

29. Glenn Beck, *Glenn Beck*, September 26, 2007.

30. Laura Ingraham, *The O'Reilly Factor*, November 19, 2007.

31. Glenn Beck, *Glenn Beck*, October 9, 2009.

32. Lou Dobbs and Lisa Sylvester, *Lou Dobbs Tonight*, April 6, 2010.

33. Sean Hannity, *Hannity & Colmes*, November 11, 2010.

34. Lou Dobbs, *Lou Dobbs Tonight*, October 8, 2007.

35. Glenn Beck, *Glenn Beck*, October 10, 2007.

36. Bill O'Reilly, *The O'Reilly Factor*, July 31, 2002.

37. Glenn Beck, *Glenn Beck*, November 28, 2007.

38. Lou Dobbs, *Lou Dobbs Tonight*, May 23, 2007.

39. Lou Dobbs, *Lou Dobbs Tonight*, October 27, 2007.

40. Merolla, Ramakrishnan, and Haynes, "'Illegal,' 'Undocumented,' or 'Unauthorized.'"

41. Chris Haynes, "How Lack of Immigrant Contact Heightens Empathy's Positive Effect on Support for Immigration Policies" (paper presented at the 28th meeting of the Politics of Race, Immigration, and Ethnicity Consortium, University of California, San Diego, CA, May 4, 2012).

FIVE

Racialized "Illegality"

The Convergence of Race and Legal Status among Black, Latino/a, and Asian American Undocumented Young Adults

Caitlin Patler

Interviewer: Have you ever hidden your immigration status from anyone?

Respondent: No. Just from strangers. . . . I'm pretty comfortable with my immigration status but I'm not going to scream it around.

Adelina, twenty-one years old, from Mexico

Interviewer: Have you ever had to hide your family's or your immigration status from anybody?

Respondent: Yeah, of course. I would say anybody—from students at my school to teachers to neighbors. A lot of people.

Interviewer: Why did you feel like you had to do that?

Respondent: Cause I don't want to have my mom . . . or my younger sisters being unsafe. . . . I just don't want to have to go over that line. I don't have the chance to stop [others] from screwing with us if they have the opportunity.

Jayson, twenty years old, from Mongolia

Respondent: When I was in high school I was asked to [fill out some forms], when they ask you about your family and stuff. I didn't want to give no information out.

Interviewer: Why not?

Respondent: 'Cause my family, they'd say "don't be telling anyone [about your immigration status], they're not gonna help you . . . things are supposed to stay in the family.". . . Like I said, I knew some [people from my country] there [at my high school] but a lot of them, a lot of them had papers from their families.

Benjamin, eighteen years old, from Belize[1]

Based on structured and unstructured interviews with more than seventy undocumented young adults from various racial groups, as well as over a decade of participant observation in immigrants' rights organizations across Southern California, this chapter seeks to provide a preliminary answer to the question: how do undocumented youth negotiate belonging in a context of legal, political, and social exclusion, and how do these experiences vary by race? It exposes some of the diverse ways that racialization intrudes into the lives of undocumented immigrants, with implications for their well-being and incorporation.[2] Although all undocumented youth must ultimately "learn to be illegal," the paths they take can vary dramatically.[3] I analyze the intersection of legal status and race, arguing that racialization differentially affects undocumented youth from various racial backgrounds, presenting unique challenges for each group.

My research suggests that undocumented young adults from different racial backgrounds often have distinct experiences of "illegality" based on the ways in which they are racialized in the U.S. context. This chapter focuses on two contexts in which racialization interacts with legal status in ways that are different—whether subtly or overtly—for Latino/a, Asian Pacific Islander (API), and black immigrants. First, I begin by exploring school-based experiences of racialization reported by diverse undocumented youth in order to assess their simultaneous (and often conflicting) socialization into both racial and legal categories. Second, I analyze undocumented youth's strategies of coping and resistance, specifically focusing on the strength (or tenuousness) of peer and social networks to help insulate the damaging impact of racism and illegality.

This chapter adds to an emerging field of literature on undocumented 1.5-generation immigrants (those who came to the United States as children or adolescents). Empirically, it adds a new case—a preliminary study of legal status across different racial groups—to a field that has focused mainly on immigrants from Latin America. Theoretically, it aims to link the sociology of race with the sociology of law and international migration. Studies of race and ethnicity have largely failed to analyze the intersections of immigrant legal status and racialization. Likewise, studies about undocumented youth, situated most commonly in theories of integration, assimilation, and social movements, have paid little attention to the role of race in shaping the lives of undocumented youth.

In the first section of this chapter, I present a brief overview of literature from two sociological subfields: theories about the effects of immigrant legal status on undocumented young adults, and studies of race and immigrant integration. Next, I present findings from my study of undocumented young adults from different racial backgrounds across Southern California. Based on these findings, I make preliminary recommendations for how social scientists might link studies of race with studies of immigration focused on the undocumented. Finally, I end with suggestions for policymakers and community organizations that seek to better serve diverse immigrant communities.

THE IMPACT OF PROLONGED "ILLEGALITY" ON UNDOCUMENTED YOUTH

An estimated eleven to twelve million undocumented immigrants reside in the United States.[4] Of these individuals, approximately five million are under thirty years old, and around two million arrived to the United States as children.[5] Undocumented immigrants face a perplexing paradox: they share a set of constitutional protections with U.S. citizens, including many rights that allow them to set down roots and become productive members of communities, yet they remain deportable and subject to political and social exclusion. Undocumented immigrants who come to the country as children are a strong example of this paradox. While they do not have formal citizenship, they have access to a certain package of rights, including the right to attend K–12 schools.[6] Indeed, millions of undocumented immigrant children are enrolled in schools across the country. Many come to identify as "American" through a mastery of English language and participation in institutions such as schools; and they become involved in their communities.[7] However, in spite of having access to certain rights, undocumented youth face barriers to their advancement at every step.

Schools are an important site in which to contextualize the experiences of immigrant youth, given that they are considered integrating institutions and educational advancement is widely understood as a key to social mobility. Several recent empirical and review studies have begun to paint a picture of the effects and implications of legal status on undocumented students, families, and communities.[8] Focusing on Latino/a immigrants, these studies show that legal status can severely hinder mobility for the undocumented. For the children of undocumented immigrants (across legal status), fear and stigma due to parents' legal status can lead to negative developmental and educational outcomes.[9]

The work of sociologists Roberto G. Gonzales and Leisy J. Abrego has been particularly helpful in exploring the effects of legal status on undocumented Mexican and Central American immigrant youth. These scholars find that undocumented youth are extensively embedded in schools.[10] However, the impacts of legal status change as young people move through the educational pipeline and transition into adulthood where they are no longer legally protected as they are in the K–12 educational setting. In his study of undocumented Mexican young adults, Gonzales presents a framework for understanding how undocumented youth "learn to be illegal" and how this affects their transition into adulthood.[11] Many must give up on dreams and aspirations and follow life courses similar to their undocumented parents, which are often incongruous with youths' expectations for themselves.[12] Although an estimated sixty-five thousand undocumented youth graduate from high schools each year, only approximately 5–10 percent of undocumented youth are reported to go on to college.[13] However, those who do enter postsecondary education face extreme hardship. For example, in a study of 510 undocumented student leaders across California, sociologist Veronica Terriquez and I found that nearly 90 percent reported difficulty paying for college, compared to 68 percent of a random sample of Californians in the same age bracket.[14]

Legal status also causes fear and stigma in the lives of Latino/a undocumented immigrants, leading them to change the course of their daily lives to avoid detection.[15] However, Abrego finds that illegality is experienced differently by first-generation undocumented immigrants than by undocumented youth: while both groups report barriers to claims making and collective action, first-generation migrants report the salience of fear in their daily lives, and undocumented children report worrying about stigma from their peers at school.[16] This finding is logical within a context in which undocumented youth are legally allowed access to schools, but often excluded from the benefits of education. Additional literature on undocumented youth has shown that those who participate in community organizations may be more likely to be civically engaged and mobilized by their precarious circumstances to make claims for more formal inclusion.[17] Such studies demonstrate the importance of supportive peer networks and organizations in helping undocumented youth know (and fight for) their rights.

These studies have made great strides toward understanding the impact of legal status on undocumented young adults. However, many studies have focused exclusively on undocumented Latino/a immigrants. This makes sense empirically, given that much of the scholarship on undocumented youth has come from Southern California, one of the most common destinations for Latin American migrants in the United

States. Less is known about the effects of legal status on racially diverse undocumented youth, though secondary-source reports have shown, for example, that the majority of undocumented students in the University of California system are Asian immigrants and many have faced stigma around their status.

Table 5.1 displays the country of origin distribution of all undocumented immigrants in the United States. As the table demonstrates, approximately 18 percent of the undocumented population (2.2 million) comes from countries outside of Latin America. Immigrants from outside of Latin America tend to have very different modes of incorporation than Mexican and other Latin American migrants, given that their contexts of reception and exit vary greatly by human capital and economic background, as well as initial legal status upon arrival.[18] For example, many (though certainly not all) Asian immigrants have higher levels of education, pre-migration, than do immigrants from Latin America.[19] In addition, many Asian immigrants initially enter the United States with some form of legal status, and become undocumented by, for example, overstaying a visa. Finally, while undocumented immigrants from Latin America are likely to know other immigrants with similar legal statuses, this may not be the case for all groups of undocumented immigrants.

Stereotypes about immigrant groups also vary. For example, in an analysis of two waves of the Ohio Poll, sociologists Jeffrey M. Timberlake and Rhys H. Williams found that respondents ranked Asian immigrant groups most positively and Latin American and Middle Eastern groups—who they associated with illegality—most negatively.[20] The authors conclude that perceptions of group characteristics are strongly linked to national debates about undocumented immigration. Differences in modes of incorporation suggest that undocumented youth from differ-

Table 5.1. Country of Origin of Undocumented Immigrants in the United States, 2010

Country/Region of Origin	Undocumented Population (in millions)	Percentage of Total Undocumented Population
Mexico	5.6	58%
Other Latin American Countries	2.6	23%
Asia	1.3	11%
Europe/Canada	0.5	4%
Africa	0.4	3%

Jeffrey S. Passel and D'Vera Cohn, "Unauthorized Immigration Population: National and State Trends, 2010," Pew Research Center Hispanic Trends Project (February 1, 2011), http://www.pewhispanic.org/2011/02/01/unauthorized-immigrant-population-brnational-and-state-trends-2010/.

ent countries of origin and racial groups (as defined in the U.S. context) may experience their legal status in distinct ways.

THE RACIALIZATION OF IMMIGRANTS IN THE UNITED STATES

Scholarship on immigrant integration has explored the impact of racialization on immigrants and their offspring, though few studies analyze these effects by immigrant legal status. Much of this literature has focused on the ways that racism and racialization lead immigrants to either retain their ethnic identity or "blend" into the (white, middle-class) mainstream.[21] This work suggests that immigrants of color (who make up the vast majority of immigrants to the United States since 1965) are racialized when they come to the United States in ways that are distinct to this country. In essence, they learn not just what it means to be immigrants to this country, but also what it means to be a person of color within the U.S. racial order. As Timberlake and Williams show, racialization has real implications: perceptions of group characteristics of certain immigrant groups are linked to debates about undocumented immigration.[22] Latinos/as, who are most closely associated with being "unauthorized," are seen much more negatively than other immigrant groups.

Racialization also affects educational outcomes and social mobility for communities of color in the United States. In their seminal study of Mexican American immigrants across five generations, sociologists Edward E. Telles and Vilma Ortiz find that the experiences of Mexican Americans are shaped by race and racism: ethnicity continues to significantly influence language, peer networks, civic engagement, and social mobility. Importantly, Telles and Ortiz also attribute second-generation educational stagnation and decline to racialization: as the shield of immigrant optimism ceases to cushion against the impact of structural racism and racialization, educational levels decrease.[23] In addition, scholars have found that descendants of Mexican immigrants tend to retain their ethnic identities even after several generations, in large part due to racism.[24]

Other immigrant groups also experience racialization. The work of sociologist Mary C. Waters has been instrumental in exposing the damaging effects of racialization on black immigrant communities. She finds that black immigrants from Africa and the Caribbean are often shocked by the racism they face in the United States, in particular the treatment they receive when others perceive them as African American.[25] Asian immigrants and their offspring also face prejudice, discrimination, and inequality, though they are not generally portrayed as disadvantaged in the media.[26] However, the children of Asian immigrants are often burdened with two competing stereotypes: the "forever foreign" stereotype and the "model minority" stereotype, both of which marginalize their diverse experiences and uphold white privilege.[27]

Regardless of legal status, immigrants are not passive actors; indeed, they demonstrate regular acts of resistance against discrimination and unjust policies. On a larger scale, there is a substantial and expanding body of literature on the mobilization of immigrant community organizations to win policy victories for immigrants across legal statuses.[28] Though opportunities for interracial immigrants rights organizing do exist, due to structural racism (in the form of residential and occupational segregation), the possibilities for group mobilization and solidarity are often bound within ethnic communities, potentially posing challenges for interracial coalition building.[29]

On a family and community level, immigrant integration literature credits co-ethnic social networks as key sites to counteract some of the negative effects of racialization and to improve educational outcomes.[30] In other words, in mobilizing the resources of their ethnic communities, and retaining an affiliation with their immigrant identities, the children of immigrants may be able to distance themselves from the damaging effects of the U.S. racial system. As such, co-ethnic social networks become important sites of resistance and mobilization against discrimination.

This chapter seeks to provide some initial hypotheses about the interplay between race and legal status in affecting the lives of undocumented immigrant youth in California. Though these conclusions are not generalizable, I hope they provide some initial ideas for how to conceptualize the multiple positionalities of undocumented youth. I pause here to emphasize the heterogeneity of immigrant communities—including by legal status—as well as of racialized groups in the United States more broadly. I focus this chapter on the connections and interplay between race and legal status, though gender and sexuality are other master identities that could very well have an impact on my findings. Importantly, this chapter is not about ascribing cultural attributes. I make no claim that the findings I describe here are the reality for all undocumented youth from any one community; in fact, many of the experiences of "learning to be illegal" span racial groups. However, my data reveal a very real experience of racialization that is imposed on undocumented youth through institutions and structural racism. Undocumented youth are racialized in the United States in ways similar to their documented counterparts, yet this racialization interacts with immigrant legal status to affect their daily lives in distinct and profound ways. This chapter seeks to lay out these experiences in ways that may be instructive not just to academics but also to educators, policymakers and, perhaps most important, interracial organizing efforts in immigrant communities.

DATA AND METHODOLOGY

I draw from structured and unstructured interviews, as well as a decade of participatory research in several community-based organizations serving undocumented immigrants in California. I interviewed over seventy undocumented young adults between 2009 and 2012. Respondents were between the ages of eighteen and thirty; most were in their early twenties. Approximately half of the respondents were female. All respondents had attended at least one year of high school in the United States, and many were high school graduates and attended some type of postsecondary education (defined as at least one semester of community college or university), though few completed a degree beyond high school due to financial constraints imposed by their legal status.

About three-quarters of respondents identified as Latino/a within the context of U.S. racial categories, with another approximately 20 percent identifying as API, and 5 percent as black or African American. These sample sizes are too small to allow broad generalizations, yet they can still be instructive to theories about the interplay between race, racialization, and legality. Most respondents live in Southern California (Los Angeles, Ventura, Orange, Riverside, and San Bernardino counties). This local context is important, given Southern California's high density of immigrant communities, as well as its minority-majority demographics. Future research in other locations will help to test whether my preliminary hypotheses are shaped by this unique geographic context.

Respondents were primarily recruited through a snowball sampling method initiating with members of undocumented youth organizations. Although not all respondents are organizational members themselves, by virtue of their networks, they may have more access to information about resources available to undocumented youth than other unauthorized immigrants in the same age group who are completely unaffiliated with organizations. In addition, I conducted eighteen interviews as a graduate student researcher for the California Young Adult Study.[31] Interviews lasted from forty-five minutes to well over two hours. I followed a general interview protocol with questions about family, high school and postsecondary experiences (civic engagement and academic), work experiences, and immigrant background. All structured interviews were recorded and transcribed, and were coded and analyzed using Dedoose software. (See appendix for abridged in-depth interview protocol.)

FINDINGS

My research suggests that undocumented young adults from different racial backgrounds have distinct experiences of "illegality" based on the ways in which they are racialized in the United States. In this section, I discuss two contexts—schools and social networks—in which legality and racialization interact in distinct ways for Latino/a, API, and black immigrants. Racialization occurs in schools, as immigrants perceived as Latino/a, API, or African American report differential treatment by teachers and counselors. Additionally, undocumented young adults, like all racialized young people, come to learn the stereotypes about the racial categories in which they are placed in the U.S. context.[32] While many of these stereotypes are damaging, some include an association with illegality, which can lead to hyper-criminalization and enhanced scrutiny.[33] Finally, undocumented immigrant youth, like their documented peers, are sorted into peer groups, and these networks provide different types of support, strategies of resistance, and stigma for unauthorized young people.

Schools and Stereotypes

Schools are a key institution for the socialization of children, regardless of background. However, as the literature mentioned has shown, racialized minority youth and low-income youth experience the school context in different ways from their more privileged peers. The undocumented youth in my sample described their experiences with racialization in ways that align with much of the literature on race.[34] Latino/a and black undocumented students reported that teachers had low expectations of them due to their race, which frustrated them and held them back academically. Asian students reported an escalated expectation of achievement from teachers, yet they found this to be oppressive since it left little room for their experiences as undocumented youth from low-income families. In addition, Latino/a respondents regularly reported being perceived by others as undocumented; Asian and black respondents did not report such stereotypes.

Many of the Latino/a youth I interviewed reported discrimination from peers, teachers, and counselors alike. For example, Enrique came to the United States from Mexico at fourteen years old and entered high school as an English-language learner. He recounted his experience meeting with his guidance counselor on the first day of ninth grade:

> This is like the first day of high school that she tells me . . . "yeah, don't worry, you're Hispanic so you're going to take ten years to graduate, so it's ok. Or at least the majority of you won't graduate." To me it was a little bit insulting, but I didn't say anything because she's my authority, so if I disrespect her, I get in trouble. So I don't want to get in trouble on my first day of school.

Because Enrique had come to the United States as an adolescent, he vividly recalled his experience crossing the border, and therefore knew from his first day in the country that he was undocumented. Due to his immigration status and respect for "authority," Enrique tried hard not to "get in trouble" in school. However, the counselor's stereotype of Enrique affected his educational outcomes, in particular the classes he was allowed to enroll in.

> The first couple years [of high school] it wasn't very good . . . the same counselor kept giving me—and I'm sorry [to use this language]—but the "bullshit classes.". . . I was just doing ceramics for two full semesters. Instead of taking any other classes, I was doing ceramics. Partly because I probably didn't know enough English, but also the counselor didn't want to give me any more classes besides that.[35]

This experience was particularly disempowering for Enrique because he repeatedly asked the counselor to help him enroll in higher-level courses.

Experiences with unsupportive school personnel were common among respondents. For example, respondents told story after story of counselors who were unconcerned about their progress to begin with, but then shunned students further when they came for support around legal status. Most counselors were under-informed (and many were completely uninformed) about laws and policies, such as California's in-state tuition law, Assembly Bill (AB) 540.[36] Instead of seeking help or information for the students, many counselors advised them to give up on the idea of higher education altogether. Several students recounted that they found out separately about AB 540 and often had to teach counselors and administrative personnel about the policy, facing criticism and snub from some of these individuals. Felicia, a twenty-year-old undocumented student from Mexico, described being "humiliated" when she went to the financial aid office at her local community college to ask about AB 540. She recalled that the woman working at the window had no idea about the policy and began to question Felicia, looking at her skeptically. After noticing all the students in line behind her craning their necks to hear the disagreement, Felicia left the office in tears.[37] Experiences like Felicia's and Enrique's were recounted by many Latino/a respondents, especially those who were not high-performing students. Although current college students tended to recall at least one supportive counselor or teacher as helpful on their path to college, respondents regularly described teachers and school personnel as having "low expectations" of them and of Latinos/as in general.

While racist stereotypes about Latinos/as affect immigrants and non-immigrants alike, the situation worsened when harmful racial stereotypes interacted with the disadvantages imposed by legal status. When asked about whether or not anyone had ever assumed that they were undocumented based on their race, Latino/a undocumented youth were overwhelmingly likely to answer affirmatively. They regularly described being accused or targeted for being undocumented, especially by peers but also, on occasion, by teachers, counselors, and other school personnel. Many also felt that the Latino community in general was much more likely to be presumed to be undocumented due to negative media portrayals of unauthorized migration and unauthorized immigrants.[38] Jaime, a twenty-year-old undocumented university student from Mexico, told me:

> I have gone through a lot of those experiences [with discrimination] . . . because at moments [people] tend to say things because that's the only thing they know about. For example, my immigrant status, the only thing they relate it to is what they see in the media and what they hear from other people. They don't hear from the people who are going through this process of being undocumented, just trying to improve their living conditions. In school some of my peers had families who were undocumented but they weren't really educated about the issue and they were making assumptions that weren't real.[39]

Felicia shared an additional experience of being targeted for being perceived as undocumented. "I was walking by downtown L.A. and there was this African American guy riding his bicycle and I was walking slowly with my brother and he said 'move wetback.'" Felicia described being confused about who the man was talking to, but then realized he was addressing her: "I was like, 'probably he said that to another person,' but I looked around and I was the only one [on the street]."[40] As a student, Felicia was surprised to be perceived as undocumented, yet this experience suggested that she was not exempt from these damaging stereotypes.

Asian respondents described different experiences with racialization and discrimination. John is a twenty-one-year-old undocumented young man originally from South Korea who had become undocumented after his father's visa expired. John did not know anyone else who was undocumented and he was scared to tell his teachers and counselors about his legal status. He said that all his counselors "expected" him to go to college. Part of this was because of his good grades and extracurricular participation, but he cited the "model minority myth" as also having an impact on this treatment by teachers. He recounted that teachers "automatically" expected him to do well: "because of my race they assumed I was 'good at math' and things like that."[41]

Many undocumented Asian respondents echoed this experience. Samuel (a twenty-four-year old from Indonesia) and Janice (a twenty-one-year old from South Korea) also reported that they felt that they were "expected" to do well in school because of their race.[42] However, though the model minority stereotypes might have kept teachers from assuming underachievement, it did so at the cost of homogenizing all those racialized as Asian. As a result, undocumented Asian respondents tended to feel particularly isolated due to their status and the challenges it imposed. Teachers' assumptions that all Asian Americans are *not* disadvantaged served to silence the experiences of students from undocumented families who remain in poverty due to the barriers imposed by their status.[43]

In addition to experiences in the classroom, some Asian undocumented respondents cited experiences where they were perceived as racially homogenous and altogether foreign, though not necessarily undocumented. Samuel shared this experience.

> It was a two-week summer camp [out of state] and we went to Wal-Mart to buy supplies and I was with my white friends . . . and then this white guy, he was behind me, and he takes his cart and he pushes it—like smashes it—into my cart. I almost hurt my pinky because where he hit, it almost took off my pinky. And he's like, "go back to China you Chink." And I was furious because I was like, "I'm not from China, you asshole." Then it kind of caused a commotion and my white friends, they all jumped in and were like "calm down, it's cool." But no, it's not cool. . . . I think my experience helped me to remember that I am a minority in America.[44]

After Samuel finished telling me this story, he told me that although the man had assumed that he was an immigrant, his ignorance appeared to be based in racism but not directly related to assumptions about legal status.

Undocumented Asian respondents frequently reported that they had rarely or never been in situations where they were assumed to be undocumented. For example, Esther, a twenty-four-year-old South Korean undocumented immigrant, told me: "certain Korean people get discriminated because they look a little bit more Korean," but, like Samuel, credited that to discrimination based on race, not legal status. She added, "No, I don't think that people ever assume I am undocumented because of my race."[45]

Black undocumented immigrants reported experiences with racialization in two ways. First, like their Latino/a counterparts, undocumented black students struggled with unsupportive teachers and counselors. Jeremiah, born in Panama, is twenty-three years old. He identifies with both black and Latino communities, but told me he is often perceived as African American. He recalled his high school guidance counselor's low expectations for him: "They were trying to put me in art [classes], you know, just to graduate. I didn't know that I could take anything else, you know. I didn't even know about the A-G [California college admissions] requirements." Although black undocumented respondents recounted regular instances of racism and discrimination, they reported few situations in which they were perceived to be undocumented. Jeremiah also shared his experience with unsupportive guidance counselors at his community college: "I don't think they cared about us. . . . I used to have braids. I used to have long hair . . . and I think—and you see the way I'm dressed. I just look like a regular street kid." I then asked him, "You think they were discriminating?" to which he responded "I really do think they were. I really think that they would see me come in and just be like, 'This kid's not going nowhere. Here, just take these little few classes, and you'll probably drop out in a couple years.'"[46]

Second, in an alternative display of anti-black racism, black undocumented youth also reported that teachers began to treat them differently once they found out they were not born in the United States. Respondents recalled being treated as "exceptional" after teachers discovered that they were immigrants. Benjamin, from Belize, recounted how his teachers began to encourage him to do well because he was "not like the other [native-born] kids." He said that although he ended up dropping out of high school and attending a continuation school, teachers in both institutions were always supportive of him and encouraged him.[47]

Peer and Social Networks

Supportive peer and social networks are theorized to shield immigrant children from some of the more damaging effects of racialization in the U.S. context and contribute to their mobility.[48] However, for undocumented youth in my sample, the level of racial isolation of peer networks also determined access to support and resources specifically related to legal status. On the one hand, undocumented Latinos/as reported being relatively open about their legal status among their peer groups, due to the fact that many in their co-ethnic social network could relate to the challenges of legal status. This allowed them to access information and resources that could help them confront the barriers imposed by their legal status. On the other hand, undocumented black and Asian young people tended to report feeling isolated in their co-ethnic social networks, and too scared or embarrassed to seek support related to their legal status.

Latino/a respondents who reported a peer group made up mostly of co-ethnics or of other undocumented people were much more likely to be open about their status among friends. I asked Ivette, a nineteen-year-old undocumented Latina from Mexico, about her friendship group, and she said that although she was the only undocumented immigrant in her immediate group of friends, she felt comfortable talking about her status because others in her racial group could empathize with her situation: "Some of my friends are Hispanics. And Hispanics, one or two of their family, they don't have papers. Like their parents. Maybe they were born here—or their siblings—but their parents were not, so they can understand. I feel more comfortable with people that can understand me."[49] In this case, Ivette felt that her friends could understand her because of their shared ethnic background.

Because undocumented Latino/a students tended to know more people in the same precarious legal situation, they were also more likely to participate in organizations aimed at helping undocumented students. Through these organizations, they were able to receive emotional support, access information about resources, and become involved in leadership development and even political activities. Indeed, organizational participation can be extremely empowering and rewarding, providing undocumented students a new way to view their status. Jaime, an immigrant from Mexico, stated:

> You have to look at the positive side of all the experiences that we go through, all of these struggles. I've said it always to other students . . . that being undocumented has been one of the greatest things that has ever happened to us in our lives. The first time I said that, they looked at me weird and some students didn't agree with me. But again, it's the way you look at things, and reality, if we had not been in this situation we wouldn't be talking right here and all of this movement wouldn't exist. And believe me, all of this that we're learning or that we have learned, it's a lesson for life and it's something that we're going to pass on to our children, to another generation, because it's a lesson of life.[50]

In contrast, many black and Asian immigrants did not feel comfortable revealing their status to their peers. Jeremiah came to the United States from Panama as a child. He was the only undocumented person in his family and the majority of his friends were native-born. No one else he knew could relate to his situation. He confessed to me that he had never told *anyone* in high school or college about his status, and even refrained from participating in activities because of it: "I was never really trying to get involved that much at the school. . . . I didn't trust nobody, so I didn't ever try to do anything. I was just trying to go to school, get my education and get out." Jeremiah described his life in high school as a "web of lies" that he felt he had to tell to avoid discovery. "To tell you the truth, I've been lying for a long time . . . even my best friend—my best friend ever since preschool, I didn't even tell him until a year or two ago. . . . Yeah, it's like, I would think that would be my best friend and I would tell him, but I'm just so embarrassed of it."[51] Although some of his friends now know about his status, Jeremiah still keeps his head down and his status hidden. As quoted in the opening section of this chapter, Benjamin, born in Belize, also reported feeling unable to talk about his status in his peer group: "I knew some [people from my country] there [at my high school] but a lot of them, a lot of them had papers from their families."[52] As a result, Benjamin felt that there was no one he could talk to about his status.

Asian undocumented immigrants reported similar experiences. Although many spent time in co-ethnic social groups, they were uncomfortable revealing their status. As Samuel said, "I know there have been some

Asians that are more understanding, but when it comes to undocumented status it's something you don't say, it's just, you don't talk about it." Colleen, a twenty-one-year-old undocumented university student from South Korea, told me I was the first person she had ever told about her status. During our interview, she cried several times, telling me how hard it was to feel like she was the only one in her situation.[53]

Unfortunately, the isolation of black and Asian undocumented youth often leads to a lack of information about the resources available to undocumented students. Though support groups for undocumented immigrants have emerged throughout the state, these organizations tend to have been founded by Latino/a students and serve mostly Latino/a members.[54] As a result, although undocumented student organizations generally seek to be inclusive spaces for diverse immigrants, non-Latinos/as often reported being worried that they would not fit in within these organizations.

CONCLUSION

As this exploratory study has revealed, undocumented immigrant youth from diverse backgrounds face multiple levels of oppression. They often spend a large part of their childhood in U.S. schools and therefore experience the same detrimental racialization as their native-born peers. However, they face an additional set of barriers due to their status. Latino/a respondents in particular describe being perceived as undocumented. Although most undocumented youth have friends from various ethnic groups, due to racial segregation in their schools and communities, their peer networks tend to be fairly homogenous. They are therefore differentially exposed to emotional support about their status as well as access to information about resources available to undocumented youth.

These preliminary conclusions have implications for educational and immigration policy, as well as efforts for multiracial organizing. From a policy perspective, though recent legislation granting undocumented students in-state tuition and increased financial aid has further opened the doors to higher education, these laws are consistently challenged. They must be protected so that undocumented students are not excluded from access to social mobility. In addition, more formal programs need to be put in place to educate teachers, counselors, and school personnel on how to better serve undocumented children. It is unacceptable that more than twelve years after the passage of AB 540, students still report that guidance counselors do not know about the law's existence and continue to tell undocumented students that they cannot go to college.

However, educational policies only go so far. AB 540 and even limited access to financial aid do not fundamentally alter existing power structures in this country. The fact remains that most undocumented families live in poverty, work in exploitative jobs, and are systematically kept in fear due to the "legal violence" imposed on them by restrictive immigration laws.[55] Politicians must heed the call of immigrant-led organizations and make the difficult but important choice to address the real roots of poverty and oppression.

In spite of constantly living in state-enforced liminal legality, immigrant communities (undocumented and otherwise) have demonstrated time and time again that they are not passive actors.[56] Indeed, immigrant organizations have built enough power to change the debate on immigration and immigrants' rights in this country.[57] However, multiracial organizing has sometimes proven difficult, often due to the racist power structures that pit diverse groups against one another in competition for scarce resources.[58] The experiences of undocumented youth highlighted in this chapter suggest that organizations serving undocumented youth should continue to find ways to reach out to individuals from many different backgrounds. This is an effort already underway by many groups across the country. For example, the DREAM Resource Center of the UCLA Labor Center hosts a DREAM Summer Internship for activists in the immigrant youth movement. In 2013, the program hosted interns focused specifically on expanding the movement to underrepresented groups of undocumented youth including API and queer leaders.[59] Programs such as these have great potential to open the doors to support and provide resources for undocumented youth from many different backgrounds.

APPENDIX 5.1

Abridged In-Depth Interview Protocol

A. Background and Education

- Could you tell me about the neighborhood (in the United States) where you spent most of your teenage years?
- Who raised you?
- Where (in what city, country) did you go to elementary school and middle school?
- Could you describe the high school you went to? What was the racial/ethnic background of the students? Were they mostly immigrants? Were they middle, low, or high income? How could you tell?
- Are you currently enrolled in school? Have there been any barriers that have kept you or might have kept you from continuing your education?

- Some people tell us that they have felt like they were treated unfairly at school due to certain personal characteristics like race, sex, sexuality, national origin, religion, language abilities, or immigration status. Do you feel you have ever been treated unfairly at school by peers, teachers, administrators, or anybody else? If so, can you tell me what happened?

B. Employment

- Are you currently employed?
- Some people tell us that they have felt like they were treated unfairly at work (or when looking for a job) due to certain personal characteristics like race, sex, sexuality, national origin, religion, language abilities, or immigration status. Do you feel you have ever been treated unfairly at work (or when looking for a job) by employers, coworkers, customers/clients, or anybody else?
- What career would you want to have in the next ten years or so?
- Has your immigration status ever been a barrier in looking for employment?

C. Civic Engagement

- Are you involved in any political, religious, community, student, or volunteer organizations?
- What do you do in your spare time? Who do you hang out with? Are you usually around people who are from the same background as you?

D. Immigrant Experience

- How old were you when you came to the United States? Can you tell me a little about your first experiences in the United States?
- When you were a child, what language did you speak at home? Do your parents speak English now?
- Do you have any children or other financial dependents? Were they born in the United States?

E. Self-Perception

- Some people tell us that they feel sad sometimes when they think about the challenges their families face because they are immigrants, especially if they are undocumented. What kinds of challenges do you think immigrant families face? What impact do these challenges have on their life trajectories? On their self-esteem? Has your family faced any of these difficulties?
- When did you first start to think about your immigration status?

- How comfortable do you feel about telling people about your status? Does anybody outside of your family know about your status? What kinds of things do you consider when deciding whether or not to tell someone? Have you ever hidden your status from anyone?
- Has your status ever impacted your social or personal life?

F. For All

- Some people tell us that there are stereotypes about their racial group. What are some of the stereotypes about your racial group? Have you ever felt discrimination based on your race? Are there any stereotypes about *immigrants* in your racial group? What are they? Do you think people ever assume you are undocumented because of your race? Can you give me examples of any of this?
- If you had to name a few of the advantages of being an immigrant to the United States, what would you say?

NOTES

1. Adelina, interview by author, Los Angeles, September 2, 2010; Jayson, interview by author, Torrance, CA, September 30, 2010; and Benjamin, interview by author, Los Angeles, October 3, 2010. All names and other identifying information have been changed to protect the privacy of respondents. I gratefully acknowledge support from the National Science Foundation (grant # DGE-0707424), Ford Foundation, University of California Institute for Mexico and the United States, University of California Center for New Racial Studies, and UCLA Institute for Research on Labor and Employment. Parts of this chapter were presented at the 2011 Law and Society Association Annual Meeting in San Francisco, California. My thanks go to Veronica Terriquez for providing access to data from the California Young Adult Study. I also thank Maria Abesa, Carlos Amador, Jose Beltran, Alma Castrejon, David Cho, Samantha Contreras, Deisy Del Real, and Fabiola Santiago for their outstanding research assistance. I am truly indebted to the dozens of undocumented youth who shared their stories with me; you remain my daily inspiration.

2. "Racialization" refers to the sorting of individuals into a social hierarchy based on meanings of presumed physical and cultural characteristics.

3. Roberto G. Gonzales, "Learning to Be Illegal: Undocumented Youth and Shifting Legal Contexts in the Transition to Adulthood," *American Sociological Review* 76 (2011): 602–19.

4. Jeffrey S. Passel and D'Vera Cohn, "Unauthorized Immigration Population: National and State Trends, 2010," Pew Research Center Hispanic Trends Project (February 1, 2011), http://www.pewhispanic.org/2011/02/01/unauthorized-immigrant-population-brnational-and-state-trends-2010/.

5. Karina Fortuny, Randolph Capps, and Jeffrey S. Passel, *The Characteristics of Unauthorized Immigrants in California, Los Angeles County, and the United States* (Washington, DC: The Urban Institute, 2007).

6. *Plyler v. Doe*, 457 U.S. 202 (1982) upheld access to K–12 public education, regardless of legal status.

7. On schools, see William Perez, *We ARE Americans: Undocumented Students Pursuing the American Dream* (Sterling, VA: Stylus Publishing, 2009). On communities, see Veronica Terriquez and Caitlin Patler, "Aspiring Americans: Undocumented Youth

Leaders in California," *Center for the Study of Immigrant Integration Publications* (June 2012), http://csii.usc.edu/documents/AspiringAmericans_web.pdf.

8. Frank D. Bean, Susan K. Brown, M. A. Leach, and J. D. Bachmeier, "Parental Pathways: How Legalization and Citizenship among Mexican Immigrants Relates to Their Children's Economic Well-being" (paper presented at the annual meeting of the American Sociological Association, Boston, MA, July 31, 2008); Katharine M. Donato and Amada Armenta, "What We Know about Unauthorized Migration," *Annual Review of Sociology* 37 (2011): 529–43; Gonzales, "Learning to Be Illegal"; and Perez, *We ARE Americans.*

9. Carola Suárez-Orozco, "Identities under Siege: Immigration Stress and Social Mirroring among the Children of Immigrants," in *Cultures under Siege: Collective Violence and Trauma,* eds. Antonius C. G. M. Robben and Marcelo M. Suárez-Orozco (Cambridge: Cambridge University Press, 2000), 194–226; Carola Suárez-Orozco, Hirokazu Yoshikawa, Robert T. Teranishi, and Marcelo M. Suárez-Orozco, "Growing Up in the Shadows: The Developmental Implications of Unauthorized Status," *Harvard Educational Review* 81 (2011): 438–73; Marcelo M. Suárez-Orozco, *Crossings: Mexican Immigration in Interdisciplinary Perspectives* (Cambridge, MA: Harvard University Press, 1998); Hirokazu Yoshikawa, *Immigrants Raising Citizens: Undocumented Parents and Their Young Children* (New York: Russell Sage Foundation, 2011); and Hirokazu Yoshikawa and Niobe Way, "Beyond the Family: Contexts of Immigrant Children's Development," *New Directions for Child and Adolescent Development* 121 (2008): 1–104.

10. Leisy J. Abrego, "Legitimacy, Social Identity, and the Mobilization of Law: The Effects of Assembly Bill 540 on Undocumented Students in California," *Law and Social Inquiry* 33 (2008): 709–34; Leisy J. Abrego, "'I Can't Go to College Because I Don't Have Papers': Incorporation Patterns of Latino Undocumented Youth," *Latino Studies* 4 (2006): 212–31; Gonzales, "Learning to Be Illegal"; and Roberto G. Gonzales and Leo R. Chavez, "Awakening to a Nightmare: Abjectivity and Illegality in the Lives of Undocumented 1.5-Generation Latino Immigrants in the United States," *Current Anthropology* 53 (2012): 255–81. See also Perez, *We ARE Americans.*

11. Gonzales, "Learning to Be Illegal."

12. Abrego, "I Can't Go to College"; Roberto G. Gonzales, "Wasted Talent and Broken Dreams: The Lost Potential of Undocumented Students," *Immigration Policy in Focus* 5 (2007): 1–11; Gonzales, "Learning to Be Illegal"; and Immigration Policy Center (IPC), American Immigration Council, "The DREAM Act: Creating Opportunities for Immigrant Students and Supporting the U.S. Economy" (2010), http://www.immigrationpolicy.org/just-facts/dream-act.

13. On high school graduation rates, see Jeffrey S. Passel, "Further Demographic Information Relating to the DREAM Act" (Washington, DC: The Urban Institute, 2003), http://www.nilc.org/document.html?id=20; and for college attendance, see IPC, "The DREAM Act."

14. Terriquez and Patler, "Aspiring Americans," 3.

15. Susan Bibler Coutin, *Legalizing Moves: Salvadoran Immigrants' Struggle for U.S. Residency* (Ann Arbor: University of Michigan Press, 2000); Nicholas P. De Genova, "Migrant 'Illegality' and Deportability in Everyday Life," *Annual Review of Anthropology* 31 (2010): 419–47; Cecilia Menjívar and Leisy J. Abrego, "Legal Violence: Immigration Law and the Lives of Central American Immigrants," *American Journal of Sociology* 117 (2012): 1380–1421; and Guillermina Gina Nuñez and Josiah McC. Heyman, "Entrapment Processes and Immigrant Communities in a Time of Heightened Border Vigilance," *Human Organization* 66 (2007): 354–65.

16. Leisy J. Abrego, "Legal Consciousness of Undocumented Latinos: Fear and Stigma as Barriers to Claims-Making for First- and 1.5-Generation Immigrants," *Law and Society Review* 45 (2011): 337–69.

17. Terriquez and Patler, "Aspiring Americans"; Abrego, "Legitimacy, Social Identity, and the Mobilization of Law"; Carlos Amador, "This Is Our Country Too: Undocumented Immigrant Youth Organizing and the Battle for the DREAM Act," *Critical Planning* (2011): 107–14; Roberto G. Gonzales, "Left Out But Not Shut Down: Political

Activism and the Undocumented Student Movement," *Northwestern Journal of Law & Social Policy* 3 (2008): 1–22; Alejandra Rincón, *Undocumented Immigrants and Higher Education: Sí Se Puede!* (New York: LFB Scholarly Publishing, 2009); Hinda Seif, "'Wise Up!' Undocumented Latino Youth, Mexican-American Legislators, and the Struggle for Higher Education Access," *Latino Studies* 2 (2004): 210–30; and Hinda Seif, "'Unapologetic and Unafraid': Immigrant Youth Come Out from the Shadows," *New Directions for Child and Adolescent Development* 134 (2011): 5–21.

18. Philip Kasinitz, John Mollenkopf, and Mary C. Waters, *Inheriting the City: The Children of Immigrants Come of Age* (New York: Russell Sage Foundation, 2008); Alejandro Portes and Rubén G. Rumbaut, *Legacies: The Story of the Immigrant Second Generation* (Berkeley and Los Angeles: University of California Press, 2001); Alejandro Portes and Min Zhou, "The New Second Generation: Segmented Assimilation and Its Variants," *Annals of the American Academy of Political and Social Science* 530 (1993): 74–96; and Min Zhou, Jennifer Lee, Jody Agius Vallejo, Rosaura Tafoya-Estrada, and Yang Sao Xiong, "Success Attained, Deterred, and Denied: Divergent Pathways to Social Mobility in Los Angeles's New Second Generation," *Annals of the American Academy of Political and Social Science* 620 (2008): 37–61.

19. Min Zhou and Susan Kim, "Community Forces, Social Capital, and Educational Achievement: The Case of Supplementary Education in the Chinese and Korean Immigrant Communities," *Harvard Educational Review* 76 (2006): 1–29.

20. Jeffrey M. Timberlake and Rhys H. Williams, "Stereotypes of U.S. Immigrants from Four Global Regions," *Social Science Quarterly* 93 (2012): 867–90. The Ohio Poll regularly conducts phone surveys of residents in Ohio.

21. Richard D. Alba and Victor Nee, *Remaking the American Mainstream: Assimilation and Contemporary Immigration* (Cambridge, MA: Harvard University Press, 2003); Tomás R. Jiménez, *Replenished Ethnicity: Mexican Americans, Immigration, and Identity* (Berkeley and Los Angeles: University of California Press, 2010); Joel Perlmann, *Italians Then, Mexicans Now: Immigrant Origins and Second-Generation Progress, 1890 to 2000* (New York: Russell Sage Foundation, 2005); Joel Perlmann and Mary C. Waters, "Intermarriage Then and Now: Race, Generation, and Changing Meaning of Marriage," in *Not Just Black and White: Historical and Contemporary Perspectives on Immigration, Race, and Ethnicity in the United States*, eds. Nancy Foner and George M. Fredrickson (New York: Russell Sage Foundation, 2005), 262–77; and Edward E. Telles and Vilma Ortiz, *Generations of Exclusion: Mexican Americans, Assimilation, and Race* (New York: Russell Sage Foundation, 2008).

22. Timberlake and Williams, "Stereotypes of U.S. Immigrants."

23. Telles and Ortiz, *Generations of Exclusion.*

24. Ibid.; and Jiménez, *Replenished Ethnicity.*

25. Mary C. Waters, "Ethnic and Racial Identities of Second Generation Black Immigrants in New York City," *International Migration Review* 28 (1994): 759–820; and Mary C. Waters, *Black Identities: West Indian Immigrant Dreams and American Realities* (New York: Russell Sage Foundation, 1999).

26. Michael Omi, "Asian-Americans: The Unbearable Whiteness of Being," *The Chronicles of Higher Education* (September 26, 2008).

27. Ibid.; and Nazli Kibria, "Race, Ethnic Options, and Ethnic Binds: Identity Negotiations of Second-Generation Chinese and Korean Americans," *Sociological Perspectives* 43 (2000): 77–95.

28. Coutin, *Legalizing Moves*; Hector L. Delgado, *New Immigrants, Old Unions: Organizing Undocumented Workers in Los Angeles* (Philadelphia, PA: Temple University Press, 1993); Ruth Milkman, *L.A. Story: Immigrant Workers and the Future of the U.S. Labor Movement* (New York: Russell Sage Foundation, 2006); Caitlin C. Patler, "Alliance-Building and Organizing for Immigrant Rights: The Case of the Coalition for Humane Immigrant Rights of Los Angeles," in *Working for Justice: The L.A. Model of Organizing and Advocacy*, eds. Ruth Milkman, Victor Narro, and Joshua Bloom (Ithaca, NY: Cornell University Press, 2010), 71–88; and Monica W. Varsanyi, "The Paradox of

Contemporary Immigrant Political Mobilization: Organized Labor, Undocumented Migrants, and Electoral Participation in Los Angeles," *Antipode* 37 (2005): 775–95.

29. Janice Fine, *Worker Centers: Organizing Communities at the Edge of the Dream* (Ithaca, NY: Cornell University Press, 2006); Chinyere Osuji, "Building Power for 'Noncitizen Citizenship': A Case Study of the Multi-Ethnic Immigrant Workers Organizing Network," in *Working for Justice* (see note 28), 89–105; Patler, "Alliance-Building and Organizing"; and Dina G. Okamoto, "Institutional Panethnicity: Boundary Formation in Asian-American Organizing," *Social Forces* 85 (2006): 1–25.

30. Portes and Zhou, "New Second Generation"; Min Zhou and Charles L. Bankston III, *Growing Up American: How Vietnamese Children Adapt to Life in the United States* (New York: Russell Sage Foundation, 1998); and Zhou and Kim, "Community Forces, Social Capital, and Educational Achievement."

31. The 2011–12 California Young Adult Study (CYAS) explores the educational, employment, and civic engagement trajectories of California's diverse eighteen- to twenty-six-year-old population with the goal of identifying social inequalities and institutional resources that might ameliorate them. The study includes random digit dial phone surveys, web surveys, and follow-up in-depth interviews. For more on the CYAS, visit http://www-bcf.usc.edu/~vterriqu/#.

32. Waters, *Black Identities*.

33. Though I do not analyze the criminalization of young people (especially young men) of color in this chapter, these experiences have been widely documented in other research (for example, see Victor M. Rios, *Punished: Policing the Lives of Black and Latino Boys* [New York: New York University Press, 2011]). Black and Latino/a undocumented youth in particular are often subject to increased scrutiny by enforcers of discipline, both on campus and beyond. This is an especially problematic situation for undocumented young people, who, if arrested, could face serious legal consequences, including deportation.

34. Kibria, "Race, Ethnic Options, and Ethnic Binds"; Telles and Ortiz, *Generations of Exclusion*; and Waters, "Ethnic and Racial Identities."

35. Enrique, twenty-six years old, interview by author, Los Angeles, September 17, 2010.

36. Passed in 2001, AB 540 is a state law that allows undocumented students and out-of-state U.S. citizens in California to pay in-state tuition at public colleges and universities if students meet a set of criteria. For more information, see http://dreamresourcecenter.org/assembly-bill-540/.

37. Felicia, interview by author, Carson, CA, September 30, 2010.

38. On portrayals of undocumented immigrants, see Leo R. Chavez, *Covering Immigration: Popular Images and the Politics of the Nation* (Berkeley and Los Angeles: University of California Press, 2001); Leo R. Chavez, *The Latino Threat: Constructing Immigrants, Citizens, and the Nation* (Stanford, CA: Stanford University Press, 2008); Otto Santa Ana, "'Like an Animal I Was Treated': Anti-Immigrant Metaphor in US Public Discourse," *Discourse & Society* 10 (1999): 191–224; Otto Santa Ana, *Brown Tide Rising: Metaphors of Latinos in Contemporary American Public Discourse* (Austin: University of Texas Press, 2002); and Otto Santa Ana, *Juan in a Hundred: The Representation of Latinos on Network News* (Austin: University of Texas Press, 2002).

39. Jaime, interview by author, Los Angeles, August 20, 2010.

40. Felicia, interview.

41. John, interview by author, Los Angeles, August 27, 2010.

42. Samuel, interview by author, Los Angeles, October 1, 2010; and Janice, interview by author, Los Angeles, August 20, 2010.

43. Kibria, "Race, Ethnic Options, and Ethnic Binds"; and Omi, "Asian-Americans."

44. Samuel, interview.

45. Esther, interview by author, Los Angeles, August 20, 2010.

46. Jeremiah, interview by author, San Bernardino, CA, March 10, 2012.

47. Benjamin, interview.

48. Portes and Zhou, "New Second Generation"; and Zhou and Kim, "Community Forces, Social Capital, and Educational Achievement."

49. Ivette, interview by author, Long Beach, CA, December 5, 2012.

50. Jaime, interview.

51. Jeremiah, interview.

52. Benjamin, interview.

53. Samuel, interview; and Colleen, interview by author, Los Angeles, August 11, 2010.

54. Terriquez and Patler, "Aspiring Americans."

55. Menjívar and Abrego, "Legal Violence."

56. On "liminal legality," see Cecilia Menjívar, "Liminal Legality: Salvadoran and Guatemalan Immigrants' Lives in the United States," *American Journal of Sociology* 111 (2006): 999–1037.

57. Amador, "This Is Our Country Too."

58. Osuji, "Building Power for 'Noncitizen Citizenship.'"

59. For more information on the DREAM Resource Center, see http://dreamresourcecenter.org/.

II

A Grassroots Perspective on Immigration Issues through Personal Narratives

SIX

Self-Empowerment through Grassroots Efforts

Patricia Huerta

Patricia Huerta, from the grassroots organization Padres Unidos (United Parents), was scheduled to address the conference on the first day, but explained later that she was so fearful of sharing her story that she was not even able to attend the gathering. She did attend on the second day and shared her life journey. What follows is a retelling of her raw and remarkable narration of her personal and social transformation as a migrant. Huerta's example and drive led to the development of Padres Unidos, an organization that offers assistance to migrants in multiple ways to create healthy families and, in a broader sense, healthy communities. Her inspirational story provides encouragement for other migrants, especially families with children, who face the various challenges associated with coming to the United States. Huerta's narrative illustrates the usefulness of public sociology—bridging personal problems with structural issues.

Hello, I am so nervous, my hands are sweating and cold. I did not come yesterday because I was so afraid, but I am here today. I am here to share a story, my family's story, from Santa Ana. I immigrated to this country in 1976 when I was fifteen years old. I was already married; we were running from persecution after my sister Alejandra was kidnapped in Chapala, Mexico. I had just married a man who was violent, and I lived with domestic violence for fourteen years. I weighed 550 pounds as a way to protect myself from the abuse. In 1989, thank God, my husband left me; I did not have the courage to leave him. He left me with four beautiful children, some of whom you met yesterday. They are here today as well: Francisco, Patricia, Ericka, and Monica, along with my son Giovanni who was born several years after my husband's departure.

117

Shortly after he left, I also took care of and later adopted a child whose mother was deported to Guatemala. After my husband left me my journey started.

Orange County, California, is very close to the border with Mexico. Yet making the switch between homeland and a foreign country is very difficult for migrants. I spent twenty years thinking, "I'm just here temporarily, I'm going to go back home." That kept me from doing what I needed to do in order to grow and be the person who I could be. Before my husband left, I never worked outside of the home. Once he was gone, I had to find work. One day I was crying in one of the pews in a small church, Sacred Heart Mission Chapel (part of St. Justin Martyr), in Anaheim, California. The priest saw me and told me, "OK, you already put all your tears all over my pews, and now you have to come and clean them up on Saturday." I went back on the following Saturday, and he invited me to become a catechist. Within three months, I was coordinating the church's program for religious education. We started with eighty parents and the numbers quickly rose to over five hundred people. Eventually I was forced to leave this church after my former husband came back and caused a violent scene. Following this incident, I searched everywhere for work, beginning with McDonald's and Carl's Jr. (a fast food restaurant chain).

Since I had dropped out of junior high school at the age of fifteen and got married, I did not have an education and I had no interest in getting one. In addition, at 550 pounds, nobody wanted to hire me. I probably filled out between 100 and 150 applications. My children and I were homeless for four months. We lived in a car with all of our possessions, which was not much. I said to my children, "we don't have a job, we don't have food, we can go back to your abusive dad, if that is what you want." Little Francisco said, "Mom, what do we have? You are the best cook in the world." Francisco, my youngest, was six years old then, the oldest was twelve. And then Patricia said, "Mom, we can sell what you make. We can make it without dad." I said, "If you support me, I will make it happen."

Because we did not have any money, in those days I fed my kids what I found in dumpsters. And it was while searching in those dumpsters that I promised myself that I was going to come out okay. So, in 1989 to 1991, we made tamales on Saturdays and sold them door by door. We also found stuff to recycle to make extra money. At the same time, we started to deliver the newspaper *The Register* at four o'clock in the morning. Because I was a victim of abuse, sexual and physical abuse, I did not want to leave my kids with anybody. The last thing I wanted was to leave my kids vulnerable to any harm. So I told them, "OK, we will get up at four o'clock. We will go and deliver the newspaper; we will come back at seven o'clock. We will get ready, you guys will go to school and I will go to school too." I picked them up from school after two o'clock. By collecting recycling, making and selling tamales, and delivering newspapers, we made it through the first two years of our journey. It was tough, but even now, when I ask my kids about the best times that we had as a family, they recall this time.

While trying to make ends meet, in 1990, I also went back to school. I remember a counselor from Cypress College said to me, "Do you want to do this? Do you want to go to school?" I said, "Yes." "OK," he said, "you will make it." In my first semester, since I did not speak the language, I got straight Fs. My kids said, "Well, let's try it again." I learned the language within six months. One semester, while I was at Cypress College, my books were stolen. I went to the director of the Extended Opportunity Programs and Services and said, "I have to drop out because my books were stolen and I do not have money to replace them." He called the police; the school police verified my story, checked my grades, and did not allow me to drop out. The director replaced all of my books. He said, "The only thing I am going to ask you is to come every semester to show me your grades. And the day of your graduation I want to be there." He has come every step of the way to congratulate me on my accomplishments. Eventually, I finished a master's degree in social work from California State University, San Bernardino. I graduated with honors, at the top of my class.

I have been working in the Santa Ana community for the past thirteen years. At first, I worked through the diocesan parenting programs, teaching parenting classes with my family. Lots of other troubled families and kids saw the way my children and I dealt with our desperation. They started to ask us how we managed. In these classes, I shared my story with parents; I talked about the struggles that we endured as immigrants. My kids talked to other kids—teenagers, elementary school kids, and one- to five-year-olds. The parents who came and listened were poor. Our programs blossomed. We started these classes with thirty people, then sixty, and then seventy. We understand where these people are coming from because we have been there too.

After I earned my master's degree, I began to work with Orange County in a branch of Children and Family Services. We took our program throughout the county until August 2011. Because of budget cuts, the county decided to split the parenting component from the kids' component. And we said no thank you. We did not want to divide the two parts, because we knew that they worked well together. So I left the county position in August 2011.

These experiences in both the diocese and the county along with the ongoing questions that I received from immigrant families about my family's journey gave birth to Padres Unidos, a great gift that I have received from God. Today, at this conference, we are joined by thirty students from Padres Unidos. Most of those present do not even speak English. They include kids who are homeless; kids who live on the streets. Some have only a second-grade education. But all of them are trying to do something for themselves and to deal with their own desperation.

We were able to form this group and to continue our efforts because of the support we receive from all the parents who have attended our classes. Not too long ago, these parents, our students, were talking about their problems and their pains, and now they are trying to give back. We need the support, we need the help, and we need to stand up and give back to our community. We not only are recipients but also contributors.

Chapman University became involved in Padres Unidos through Dr. Suzanne SooHoo, Don Cardinal, and the College of Educational Studies. They heard about Judith Magsaysay, the former director of Pio Pico Elementary School in the Santa Ana Unified School District. They visited our sites, including one of the elementary schools. They loved it and are now giving these parents—who were rejected by society because they did not have degrees, because they did not have the little paper to do what they do—extended education through Chapman. They gave us the opportunity to train, certify, and support these parents. That is why we are here. We are here because we care and because you care too. So I want to say, "Thank you." Thank you to our community; we serve 1,600 parents and kids for many, many hours every year. With only one paid social worker (I am the only one who gets paid), 1,600 people can come weekly to talk to each other about their struggles, their challenges, and a way out.

I would like to thank Blanca Lozoya, the CFO and cofounder of Padres Undios. She has been instrumental. When one of the lead agricultural companies in Orange County of California heard that we were going to be without a space to do our work, they rented a house to us right on the corner of Santa Ana and Garfield Boulevards, to have as the headquarters. And the Santa Ana Unified School District has kept using that space as a parenting support center in the elementary schools. So we are flying with you together. We are working together to solve these problems from the grassroots.

I will end with a little story. This is a story that I always tell these parents. It is a story of a little donkey that one day fell into one of the water pits. The owners, who were old, said, "You know the donkey doesn't work anymore, and it is very old. We have to share whatever little we have. So why don't we use this opportunity to kill the donkey and put it to sleep?" And then they started to throw scoops of dirt into the pit. The donkey started braying harder when it realized what was going on, and then suddenly it quieted down. The owners kept saying maybe the donkey broke its legs, maybe it could not breathe anymore, and maybe it is dead already. So they kept throwing dirt in the pit. Once the hole was almost full, they realized that when they threw in the dirt, the donkey moved out of the dirt, stepped on the dirt, and waited for the next pile to come. It kept moving one bit of dirt at a time. By the time that it was time to get out and the hole was almost full, the donkey looked at the owners, jumped, and started to climb out of the hole.

In many ways this is the story of my life. It does not matter what color you are, it does not matter who you are, and it does not matter what life throws at you. People can keep throwing dirt at you, but it is up to you to keep moving. You can stay here and whine, whine, whine. Or you can shake the dirt off and use it to make your way upward. If you don't stand up on your own two feet, and you don't do what you need to do, it does not matter how much help you get. That empowerment that tells you that you can do it has to come from within. It has to come from the heart, from yourself. Having others believe in you and your potential is important too. So my message today is that we do need support, but the best help that you can give to anybody is believing in them, empowering them, and giving them their own tools so that they can dig themselves out of their desperation, now and later. Padres Unidos is just one example of how we are empowering others by giving them the tools to reach their full potential.

SEVEN

Santa Ana, California

A Geography of Compassion through Community Reflection and Action

Harold "Biff" Baker

Biff Baker, a community activist through the Episcopal Church of the Messiah, located in Santa Ana, California, shares his perspectives on the importance of combining reflection and action in effecting change at the grassroots level of communities. Using his church and the city of Santa Ana as a case study, he outlines the role that the faith community can play and has played in this process.

In his classic work *Pedagogy of the Oppressed*, first published in Portuguese in 1968, Brazilian educator and philosopher Paulo Freire described an essential dialectic between action and critical reflection constituting his sense of praxis.[1] Action without critical reflection is "mere activism," an odd phrase but one that captures the danger of simply wanting to "do something" about the problems perceived in society, without the necessary complement of thought, analysis, and research, all that is the proper realm of sociology. Both theory and praxis are necessary components in assisting a community in need. The natural informants or collaborators of a productive public sociology are what sociologist Michael Burawoy calls "counter-publics."[2] My contention is that the church (or, more broadly, the faith community) may serve as a node or nexus of counter-publics, bringing together reflection and action.

My main case study is the Episcopal Church of the Messiah, which is located in downtown Santa Ana. The church has been involved in numerous programs of community support over the last three decades.[3]

The main figure in Messiah's ventures is Father Brad Karelius, who recently retired after thirty years as rector at the church. Those benefiting from Messiah's programs are overwhelmingly Hispanic and to a significant degree undocumented immigrants. Obviously, many other organizations are doing similar or even more dramatic work (for example, tutoring programs for disadvantaged youth, gang prevention and rehabilitation programs, advocacy community groups that promote healthy communities and responsible development, and faith-based organizations that assist with basic needs of the undocumented). Messiah is just one example of a church that engages in important and greatly needed community service. I use this church, along with examples from other organizations in the area, to show how community activism reflects Freire's and Burawoy's ideas.

THE CITY OF SANTA ANA AND THE CHURCH OF THE MESSIAH AS A COMMUNITY ANCHOR

Santa Ana, an early site of Spanish settlement, is located roughly at the southern edge of the Los Angeles metropolitan area. With a population that is about 80 percent Hispanic, it has by some accounts the highest concentration of Spanish speakers in any U.S. city. Among larger U.S. cities, it is the fourth most densely populated after New York City, San Francisco, and Chicago; by persons per housing unit, however, it is in first place with 4.6, nearly twice that of New York or Los Angeles. In a study published in 2004 by the Rockefeller Institute of Government, Santa Ana was ranked first in the nation for "urban hardship," based on a composite index of employment, housing, dependents, income, poverty, and education. In three categories, it scored a perfect one hundred, meaning at or below the bottom of the scale in terms of housing, income, and education.[4]

It is no exaggeration to say that downtown Santa Ana is an inner-city environment, where the fabric of "normal" society is stressed to the breaking point. To the casual visitor, Santa Ana has a bustling, vibrant, working-class, immigrant culture, dappled with the colors and accents of the pueblo. You have to talk to its residents and visit the more depressed neighborhoods to get a glimpse of the pervasive struggle for survival and the extreme risk to which youth is exposed. In the 1980s and 1990s, gang violence surged in Santa Ana, and the city acquired a tough reputation. I remember attending a meeting in Messiah's basement one night in the mid-90s when a young man with a festering laceration on his calf staggered in. It looked just like what he said it was, a glancing bullet wound that had not been treated. Such stories are not unusual for this rough area. The history of Messiah is instructive for the special problems faced in Santa Ana. When Messiah was built in 1889, five blocks from the center of town, it looked out on an open meadow. Since then, the city (and its problems) has grown around it.

Messiah's current surroundings can be described in a tale of three traditions that reflect a vibrant immigrant culture and a compassionate community. North of the church is the French Park area, with its lovely old houses. Just before Christmas each year, the children of Messiah go on a traditional posada through this largely Spanish-speaking neighborhood. On the posada, children pretend to be Mary and Joseph and walk from house to house, singing a song asking for shelter (*pidiendo posada*). The kids have fun, as do the neighbors. This procession brings immigrants, especially children, and the larger Santa Ana community together in festive celebration.

To the east is the Logan Barrio, a historical center of Mexican American settlement. In 1992, when gang violence was near its peak, a parishioner was shot to death in front of St. Joseph's Catholic Church, which stands near the barrio entrance. The young victim died in the arms of Father Christopher Smith, who was parish priest at the time. In response to the shooting and to show his support and solidarity with the community, Father Smith reflected on how he could help the community as a spiritual leader and organized a yearly "Blessing of the Streets," with other downtown parishes participating, held on Palm Sunday. Violence has decreased in the area, but the annual tradition continues, with large Spanish-, English-, and Samoan-speaking contingents.

To the west is the gritty Civic Center area. Taller San José, an organization that works with troubled youth, is located in this quadrant. It offers job training, life skills courses, and employment programs for high-risk youth.[5] On the evening of Good Friday, a Via Crucis procession, or Way of the Cross, moves toward the Civic Center and winds south through the center of town. This is billed as a "procession to places of suffering, struggle, and hope." It stops fourteen times for brief observances: in front of a medical clinic, Taller San José, closed businesses, the jail, and government offices, among other sites. Between stations, the group sings Spanish hymns and people take turns carrying a large wooden cross. The Santa Ana Police Department provides a motorcycle escort due to the large number of people and the busy traffic, which appears somewhat incongruous with the serene picture of the procession.

A MODEL OF REFLECTION AND PRAXIS AS PRACTICED BY COMMUNITY GROUPS

The model of reflection and praxis I describe consists of three components. First, it has a prophetic view of social reality that is deeply sensitive to the dynamics of evil and good. Second, it emphasizes physical and moral integration with the community, as opposed to a bureaucratic or administrative distance. And third, it embraces an entrepreneurial spirit, by which I mean a passionate commitment to action, that is, to doing, creating, or building something new.

As an example of the prophetic view, I think of Dwight and Leia Smith, who run the Isaiah House of Orange County Catholic Worker, a progressive faith-based organization that provides food and shelter to those in need.[6] Isaiah House is a spacious, attractive house located on a pleasant, tree-lined street. It accommodates up to 120 homeless persons; the hardier reside under a tarp in the backyard, while others live inside the house, and some even on the floor of the owners' bedroom. Once I heard Dwight talk about how they understand their mission, and I was somewhat rattled. They are literalists of the Gospel: they take what Jesus says about the poor in a direct and immediate way. They are also literalists of the prophets, and see all around us a society condemned for its blind violence and greed. This prophetic vision sees social contradictions as outward manifestations of a struggle between evil and good, where, as Father Karelius so often put it, the Kingdom of Heaven is continually threatening to break through. Father Karelius and his partners, particularly the other clergy serving at Messiah, have worked faithfully to articulate and live according to this vision.

Another component of this model of reflection and praxis is the choice to be physically and morally present in a place of crisis and struggle. Close contact with people residing in that place is essential. Messiah and other downtown churches decided to stay or leave the city when Santa Ana went through changes during the last several decades. Messiah weathered the changes and continued its service to the community. Through its many important programs and services, the church has been and continues to be morally and physically present for those in need.

An entrepreneurial outlook is the final component of reflection and praxis. Good intentions, even moral courage, are not enough to make things happen. The entrepreneurial attitude, as I have witnessed at Messiah, is opportunistic, research intensive, and collaborative. It is rooted in imagination, creativity, values, and emotions. And it is practical and results oriented.

Opportunism entails looking for the greatest needs, as well as the greatest potential, in a given situation. Prior to engaging in activism, it is important to determine who needs assistance, how best to serve them, and what resources are available. Where is the pain? What is lacking most? What connections are waiting to be made? An example of this is Padres Unidos in the Diocese of Orange, California, founded by the Huerta and Lozoya families in 1996 based on their own life experiences of overcoming adversity. Their story is told in Patricia Huerta's essay, included in the present volume. The entrepreneurial outlook is also research intensive. To be successful, you have to dig deeply into facts, observations, testimony, records, and statistics in order to determine the validity of a project and the form it should take. Abundant, detailed factual material is needed to be able to ask convincingly for financial and other support. The collaborative approach is inherently connected to research. It does not have to be my idea; it is the idea that matters. If it is a great idea, the question is how can we support it, bringing our resources together to play a role in its success? A team, a "varsity squad" as Father Karelius puts it, is needed to gather information and work together. Furthermore, community groups and scholars can collaborate in the spirit of public sociology to effect social change at the grassroots level.

The entrepreneurial perspective is also rooted in imagination, creativity, values, and emotions. It has to have heart, miles and miles and miles of heart, since the road is likely to be long. The project will need to be sold and resold to many different audiences and groups that will need to believe in and support it. If Dorothy Day (the inspiration for Catholic Worker, mentioned earlier and which is now a national organization) is the patron saint of community enterprise, Father Gregory Boyle is its rock star. Father Boyle, founder of Homeboy Industries in Los Angeles (a nonprofit organization that has several programs that help youth leave gangs by providing an array of services and opportunities), exemplifies the role of an inspired leader and speaker in gathering support and resources for even the most unlikely projects.[7] The creativity and energy of such leaders as Father Boyle make important programs come to fruition.

Finally, this outlook has to be practical and results oriented. The entrepreneurial attitude has more to do with the artist's hunger for creation than one might suppose. The desire to see something new come into existence is a powerful motivation. Then, over a long period, results become visible: for example, kids off the street and doing homework on an average weekday afternoon, teenagers accepted to college, or homeless mothers who find employment or a source of income. It is important to determine the number of such success stories. To do so, one should take photographs, make videos, write articles, and tell these stories in front of a variety of audiences.

In sum, the entrepreneurial vision puts into action an innovative approach to a problem in the surrounding community; recruits partners; develops a team and framework for its success and ongoing viability; and establishes the project on an independent footing, for example, as a 501(c)(3) nonprofit organization. An excellent example of this entrepreneurial outlook in Santa Ana is Hands Together: A Center for Children (now Children and Families), a grassroots advocacy group.[8] The organization is closely tied to Messiah's vision and circumstances. The story of Hands Together began when Messiah purchased property diagonally across Bush and Civic Center Streets from the church. At that time, the facility was occupied by medical offices. Aside from the precious additional parking spaces involved, this building represented the key to a greatly expanded downtown ministry. Based on extensive research and consultation, plans were made to establish a child care center for the working poor of the neighborhood. Messiah's partners were other local groups that included the Sisters of St. Joseph of Orange, the city of Santa Ana, Taller San José, and the St. Joseph Health Care System. From the start, this project emphasized a holistic approach to the problems of low-income families, combining health, nutrition, and high-quality early childhood education. The idea was to stack the deck as much as possible for these children's success in school and in life.

It was important that the center stand on its own as an independent nonprofit, without relying on the church budget. The startup costs, however, even with generous outside support, required the congregation to raise 250,000 dollars. Messiah is not a megachurch, the congregation is small, and most parishioners are far from rich. Yet the idea for the project captured people's hearts and imaginations. (If Messiah had existed for over one hundred years at the heart of this city, maybe Hands Together was the promised child of its old age; maybe everything before now was leading up to this time and this unlikely chunk of real estate.) Amazingly, the money was raised and the center was formed in 1999. I was on the Vestry, the governing committee of the church, at the time, and I saw the amounts that fellow parishioners contributed. Middle-class families with kids in school donated tens of thousands of dollars. Today Hands Together is thriving. In bad budget years, it has to be defended with knees and elbows, but so far it has weathered crises. (Three years ago, it was secretly visited by a dignitary of the Church of England, Rowan Williams, the archbishop of Canterbury, who for over an hour played with the children on the floor.)

Along with the early childhood education center, Hands Together has branched out into other activities. One is a sophisticated bilingual family and early childhood literacy program housed in the nearby First United Methodist Church.[9] Another is Morning Garden, a community center for homeless and low-income mothers and children, housed at Messiah.[10] Mothers learn English, and are trained in healthy nutrition and life skills. What I did not know until quite recently is that these mothers make items for sale, including *pajaritos de esperanza*, little stuffed "birds of hope" that you can buy in various boutiques and use for decorations.[11] The Orange County Register published an article about Morning Garden just before Christmas, and the *pajaritos* were flying off the shelves, so to speak. The women also make other knitted and handcrafted goods that can be purchased from their website. The money that they make is helpful, but the psychological impact for some women is even more important.[12]

Father Boyle likes to use the image of a circle of kinship that expands until no one stands outside of it.[13] The notion of kinship, or perhaps more properly *Gemeinschaft* (a term put forth by the classical sociologist Max Weber in his reference to close-knit communities that predominated in more traditional societies), in this context is an important one. In reference to some of the community dynamics that I have briefly examined here, it is this sense of kinship and compassionate community that transforms relationships and attitudes and ultimately effects social change through the promotion of social justice. The study of how this emerges in a dialectical interplay between practical experience, knowledge, and action, on the one hand, and theoretical structures and insights, on the other, is eminently the concern of true public sociology.

NOTES

1. Paulo Freire, *Pedagogía del oprimido*, trans. Jorge Mellado (Mexico City: Siglo Veintiuno Editores, 2011), 69. For an English translation, see Paulo Freire, *Pedagogy of the Oppressed*, trans. Myra Bergman Ramos and Donaldo Macedo (New York: Bloomsbury Academic, 2000).

2. Michael Burawoy, "For Public Sociology," 2004 presidential address for the American Sociological Association, *American Sociological Review* 70 (2005): 4–28, esp. 7–8.

3. For more information about the Episcopal Church of the Messiah, see http://www.messiah-santaana.org/.

4. Lisa M. Montiel, Richard P. Nathan, and David J. Wright, *An Update on Urban Hardship* (Albany, NY: The Nelson A. Rockefeller Institute of Government, 2004).

5. For more information about Taller San José, see http://tallersanjose.org/ and http://www.youtube.com/user/TallerSanJoseMedia?ob=0&feature=results_main.

6. For more information about Isaiah House, see http://occatholicworker.org/ and http://www.youtube.com/watch?v=mJ40INs1uwQ.

7. For more information about Homeboy Industries, see http://homeboy-industries.org/; http://www.youtube.com/watch?v=gBMxL8i4oZY; and the award-winning film, *Father G. and the Homeboys*, dir. John Bohm (2007).

8. For more information about Hands Together, see http://handstogether-sa.org/.

9. For more information about the literacy center of Hands Together, see http://handstogether-sa.org/about/childrens-literacy-center/.

10. For more information about Morning Garden, see http://handstogether-sa.org/about/morning-garden/.

11. For more information about birds of hope, see http://www.ocregister.com/articles/anderson-332229-moms-birds.html.

12. I encourage you to watch the video on their website, especially Evangelina's speech at the end, which points to the impact that these activities have on these women. See http://handstogether-sa.org/about/morning-garden/.

13. Gregory Boyle, SJ, *Tattoos on the Heart: The Power of Boundless Compassion* (New York: Free Press, 2010).

EIGHT

A View from the Church Bells

Edward Poettgen

Reverend Edward Poettgen is an esteemed Roman Catholic priest, the pastor of Immaculate Heart of Mary Catholic Church in Santa Ana, California. The city has one of the most vibrant Latino immigrant communities in Southern California. Poettgen's heartfelt essay contributes an essential component to this volume, as public sociology goes beyond academic theory to communicate with a larger and active audience in an endeavor to establish dialogue with local citizens and community leaders, organizers, and activists. Reading his words is to walk through the streets of Santa Ana and to share in the lives of the Latino/a immigrants whom he serves.

The viewpoint I bring to this collection is my experience in seven large Catholic churches, each with over five thousand registered families, during the past thirty-two years in the cities of Anaheim, La Habra, and Stanton, and four parishes in Santa Ana. My service has been primarily, though not exclusively, to a Spanish-speaking immigrant population. Many have had no legal documentation, others came with visas that have since expired, some acquired papers as agricultural workers, and many received residential "green" cards through the Immigration Reform and Control Act of 1986, while others, whose parents came north, were born here in the United States. I have been in contact with tens of thousands of what the conference from which this collection is based termed the "faceless Latino/a immigrants." What follows are some of my thoughts about and experiences with these "faceless" people.

A VIEW FROM THE CONFESSIONAL

I begin my thoughts from the Catholic confessional. Conscious of our failures and sinfulness we Catholics have the tradition of confessing our sins to God in the presence of a priest who serves as a representative of Christ and the church community. People refrain from going to Communion at the Sunday Mass if they have committed sin against God or neighbor. For example, some Catholics will not receive Communion if they have had an argument with their spouse that week. After so many years of hearing confessions of immigrants, many of them undocumented, I make a generic observation. I have never had anyone confess that he or she crossed over the border illegally. While some speak of breaking the law and the crime committed, sometimes in moral indignation, they do not view crossing the border as sin. This may be a topic for further reflection and discussion.

FAMILY LIFE, MARRIAGE, AND DEATH

I come into contact with immigrants not just during Sunday Mass or in the confessional, but also in day-to-day events. Over the years, I have witnessed how they come together as a community and show their deep faith in the process. For example, I recall a baby child who had almost been lost during pregnancy. He also almost did not make it at birth. Then, as a four-month-old, he was in an accident during which he lost oxygen to the brain for at least five minutes. While in the hospital, the tube in his throat had clogged and he almost died and was left in a coma-like state. Tests were taken to see if there were any signs of brain activity. The doctor told the parents that their child would never wake up or have the ability to move on his own. She spoke of the heavy weight of caring for the child, the difficulties they would encounter, and the effects on their other three children. They were left with the decision of continuing or mercifully ending a hopeless life. Their response was: "We place our child in God's hands since the child is a gift from God. We place our child in your hands in order that he may live. He has already come close to death three times and yet he still lives. There must be a reason for his living. It is hard for parents to end the life of their own child. Would you be giving the same advice if this was your child?"

It has been over one month since that child was sent home to be cared for by his parents. He does not cry nor smile. He does not move his arms or legs except when arching his back. Yet something is happening to the community in which the family lives. Youth have been coming over and marveling at the fight in this little one. They go away inspired and committed to try harder as they face their own life challenges. A young woman who had separated from her husband with a hardened heart visited the home one day. Her heart melted in the presence of the child and has since reconciled and rejoined her spouse. "We can try harder if this child can try so hard."

The parents believe that the child has a purpose in life and have already seen some of the signs/*milagros*. His presence preaches louder and better than the best of preachers that we ought not take life for granted. He has problems, to be sure, and don't we all! But his parents and the greater immigrant community in which they live have great faith, as they prepare to celebrate their child's first birthday.

I have seen this faith in marriage and death as well. In our neighborhood, I was called to give the "last rites" of the church to a dying elderly lady in her home. (This is not an unusual request among the Hispanic immigrant community.) When I arrived, I was escorted to the garage where a man and a woman were spending the last days of her life. All of their possessions were housed in this garage, along with a rented hospital bed and oxygen tank system. While visiting with them I asked if there was anything else they might want besides prayers. She wanted to know if there was any way that she and her partner could be married, could be blessed in the church. Smiling, I agreed on condition that she had to find someone willing to ask her. The man then moved to her bedside and on one knee made the request. The marriage did not take place that evening. They instructed me to return the next day.

The following day when I arrived, I found a bride dressed in white in her hospital bed with her soon-to-be husband at her side along with members of their extended family. I celebrated the Mass; I listened to God's bond with his people in the scriptures; the couple exchanged their vows; we sang songs; and for the first time in years the newlyweds received Holy Communion. We had a festive reception with delicious food in the garage-turned-chapel-turned-reception hall. The most powerful words said before the family were: "I take you to be my wife/husband, I promise to be true to you in good times and in bad, in sickness and in health. I will love you and honor you all the days of my life." We all returned to the church the next week to celebrate her funeral Mass and the mystery of love that we all had shared that day.

I have found that the immigrant community of Santa Ana embraces tradition during funerals. It is certainly cheaper to have a mortuary handle the cremation, say some prayers there, and take the urn home to display. But among Hispanic immigrants, there is resistance to this efficient handling of remains. Funerary practice varies but we continue to have Latino families who want to spend extended time in celebrating the passing of a loved one. Some families hold large gatherings at the vigil and spend hours with the body. Prayers are said; remembrances are made; and bonds of unity are shared, attempted, or strained. A funeral Mass or liturgy is also offered on behalf of the deceased and for those who remain. Families, in general, prefer caskets even if they have little money to pay for the funeral. Burial of the remains (casket/urn) brings family and friends to the cemetery where prayers are offered, the body is lowered, the dirt fills the grave, the grass is reset, and the flowers are set over the resting place. It is a place to be revisited, remembered, and reverenced. From the funeral rites that bond us with our loved ones we then receive the grace to move on with them into the next chapter of our lives. These traditions are instructive for a society that rushes through funeral rites or skips them altogether and then wonders why they have no closure to the loss of a loved one.

EDUCATION, NEIGHBORHOOD, WORK, AND IMMIGRATION STATUS

In my service to the community, I have heard many stories about educational values, the importance of neighborhoods, access to work, and the obstacles facing undocumented immigrants. For example, a mother whose second language is Spanish (her first is an indigenous language of Michoacán) asked a monolingual English-speaking teacher about her child's education. The teacher replied by discussing how the child was testing, his abilities in math, and so forth. The mother stopped her to ask once again about the education of her child. After some questioning and translation, she asked a final time about her child's education. That is, did he respect his teacher? Did he get along with other children? Did he show that he had been well educated/reared? This goes back to the question of how a well-educated person ought to act in society, outside one's family's home. This mother's concern is our concern about the society we now live in. Are we well educated? Investment in education for the next generation of dreamers can only help our nation's future. Holding off from assistance means holding all of us back.

I have come to the realization that the health of a neighborhood, especially immigrant communities, often depends on the moms working together to knit their families into a web that transmits the knowledge and resources available and keeps people from falling into despair. They connect their families with agencies and organizations as well as with one another in facing the challenges of health, education, religious devotions, and value training. They keep hope alive through their great faith that God will provide some way. Their determination shows through their gathering together, their planning, and their reaching out for help. It may be an annual Townsend Street Party with a health fair sponsored by forty local organizations and agencies. It could be organizing to ensure that the mail is safely delivered to secure mailboxes. It is often demonstrated by greater participation in their local school, regardless of their legal status. Mediating groups such as neighborhood mother groups are vital to the health of an immigrant community.

My parishioners have shared many stories about their employment opportunities. Many have made the trek into South County. Starting in the 1960s, immigrants have helped to build and maintain the county's infrastructure, businesses, and homes. They have been the landscape workers who have planted trees and shrubs and laid concrete and brick. They head down on the bus to clean hotels and houses, and care for children. They attend to the elderly in convalescent and track homes. They fill orders at fast food restaurants and clean buildings at night. They are low-income workers who make it possible for these companies to flourish and for their owners to become wealthy.

Given the parish that I serve, I come across undocumented immigrants regularly and I witness the difficulties that they experience due to their immigration status. One of my parishioners is here legally and so are his five kids, including a newborn baby. But his wife is not. She is "in the process." Gaining legal status takes many years and requires lawyer's fees, as well as caution and patience with the immigration system. For this family's case, part of the process includes demonstrating that the wife's deportation would have an adverse effect on the husband and their kids. While in the United States, she cannot legally work to help the family maintain their home and ensure that it does not go into foreclosure. The kids are bright and will do well for themselves, their family, and the state. They are loved and well raised in a traditional family setting. Their mom, however, has many obstacles. She cannot, for example, fulfill her role as a loving daughter because she cannot travel to Mexico to visit her ailing father. Although she loves him and this is the time to go as her heart aches, it is just too high a price to potentially pay if she goes and tries to come back across the border.

We can connect ancient scripture to current immigration. Ancient Israel moved from slavery in Egypt into the Promised Land. This was not well received by the Jebbusites, Canaanites, and others who possessed the land. Yet hospitality was an important Near East value. The prophets judged the nation on how its people treated the orphan, the widow, and the alien. Jesus teaches and commands us to love our neighbors. Paul wrote to the people at Corinth about everyone being part of one body. He stated: "There is no Jew nor Greek, slave or freedman." He spoke about what makes us one. We should follow this example, and greet immigrants with hospitality, not isolation and condemnation. As my stories show, these are families with traditions, values, and determination.

NINE

Newfound Evangelical Support for Immigration

Alexia Salvatierra

In this informative piece, Reverend Alexia Salvatierra, member of several faith-based groups and adjunct faculty member at the New York Theological Seminary and Biola University, points to the significance of evangelical congregations and organizations in the quest for immigration reform. As she clearly demonstrates, religious institutions are intertwined with the larger movement calling for immigrant rights. Her work illustrates the importance of public sociology, showing how religious leaders, activists, and congregants work together to foster changes in policy and attitudes.

The alien who resides with you shall be to you as the citizen among you; you shall love the alien as yourself, for you were aliens in the land of Egypt: I am the Lord your God.

—Leviticus 19:34

This verse is one of ninety-two verses in the Bible that calls the people of God to welcome strangers. Other passages go as far as to remind people that angels sometimes arrive in the form of strangers; a stranger may be a source of unexpected blessing. All of the major religious traditions have authoritative texts that call for hospitality to strangers and support positive attitudes toward strangers.

For years, the Roman Catholic Church and the Interfaith Immigration Coalition (which includes most mainline denominations) have been advocating for just and humane immigration policies and comprehensive immigration reform. Christians for Comprehensive Immigration Reform, a project of Sojourners (a Christian organization with a progressive evangelical perspective), has given voice to moderate Christian leaders who share their commitment. Since 2007, the New Sanctuary movement has engaged people of faith in actively standing with and supporting immigrant families facing deportation.

The participation of faith leaders and congregations in the struggle for immigrant rights and immigration reform has provided several resources to the broader movement. First, it has offered a stable and widespread ongoing institutional network for immigration organizing that reaches both immigrants and nonimmigrants. This allows messages that support immigration reform to reach both communities over a period of time, deepening awareness and knowledge, in a context that also calls for action—embodying ethical principles in private and public decision making. In addition, faith communities are far more likely to bring immigrants and nonimmigrants into a common organization and provide a common identity than almost any other sector of society. The experience of working together on immigration reform awakens compassion and passion in nonimmigrants while giving immigrants hope. Second, religious communities provide both a moral voice for immigration reform and holistic resources to assist immigrant families. To maintain the struggle for immigration reform, immigrant families need both moral and practical support along the way. Third, religious institutions contribute a frame and message that helps the broader public to see immigrants in more positive ways; when immigrants are seen as fellow children of God, they are less likely to be perceived as alien or dangerous. When the Sensenbrenner Bill (introduced by Rep. James Sensenbrenner [R-WI]) passed the House of Representatives in December 2005 but had not yet passed the Senate, Cardinal Roger Mahoney of the Archdiocese of Los Angeles called on Catholics across the country to continue to minister to undocumented immigrants whether or not it became illegal to do so. By calling Catholics to risk their own personal safety to stand with immigrants, Cardinal Mahoney changed the public debate.

However, some faith leaders who are known for their commitment to the Bible have not been known for their commitment to immigrant rights or reform. According to a recent study by political scientist Ruth Melkonian-Hoover at Gordon College, white evangelicals overall see immigrants as more of a threat to both society and the economy than the overall sample of the American population (50.7 percent versus 35.2 percent) and are less likely than the overall sample to see immigrants as strengthening society and the economy (21.0 percent versus 40.3 percent). Hoover also notes, however, that evangelicals' perspectives on the issues can change. Among white evangelicals who say that they have heard a positive message about immigration from their pastor, the percentage of respondents who perceive immigrants as a threat drops from 50.7 percent to 26.1 percent, and the percentage who perceive immigrants as contributing to the American society and economy rises from 21 percent to 47.8 percent. While 54 percent of white evangelicals support a public policy that includes "creating a way for illegal immigrants already here to be-come citizens if they meet certain requirements," 81.5 percent of white evangelicals who have heard a positive message about immigrants from their pastor support a path to legalization. Furthermore, white evangeli-cals who worship together with immigrants are much less likely to see immigrants as a threat (19.6 percent) than white evangelicals without personal exposure to immigrants (50.7 percent).[1]

In 2006, immigrant evangelicals began to organize around immigra-tion reform. La Red de Pastores del Sur de California (an organization that represents 1,200 Pentecostal and other evangelical Hispanic immi-grant congregations in Southern California) and the National Hispanic Christian Leadership Conference were formed in response to the threat of the Sensenbrenner Bill and the corresponding wave of anti-immigrant sentiment. In 2007, La Red partnered with Clergy and Laity United for Economic Justice of Orange County (CLUE OC) to begin a project that would bring immigrant and nonimmigrant evangelical faith leaders and congregations together to respond to the pastoral crises provoked by the broken immigration system.

In 2008, fifty-seven local evangelical faith leaders gathered for a Pas-tors' Prayer Breakfast on immigration—twenty-eight were Hispanic, twenty-eight were Anglo, and one was a Korean American pastor who serves the largest multicultural Asian American congregation in the country. This meeting catalyzed the development of the Our Children project, which engages immigrant and nonimmigrant evangelical volun-teers in a prison visitation ministry to a detention center in Fullerton, California, for unaccompanied, undocumented children and youth. The Our Children project is collaboratively operated by CLUE OC and vari-ous Christian Community Development Association (CCDA) affiliates. (CCDA is a network of widely respected evangelical organizations that carry out community development activities in low-income communities and engage congregation members in service to and with the poor.) The Our Children volunteers were also trained together and met for monthly Bible studies/support groups. They were encouraged to invite other members of their congregations to the studies. These volunteers then helped to reach out to their congregations and create opportunities for education on immigration.

The Our Children project led to the Loving the Stranger network, which engages six immigrant and nonimmigrant megachurches in active partnership (as well as several smaller evangelical congregations). The network has organized public events for the National Day of Prayer and has trained volunteers for legislative advocacy, using an original model of faith-rooted organizing and biblically based public policy advocacy.

During the same period, other evangelical efforts in different parts of the country experienced similar results. Matthew Soerens and Jenny Hwang of World Relief, and M. Daniel Carroll R., a professor at Denver

Seminary, published seminal texts on the biblical rationale for supporting immigration reform.[2] World Relief staff worked closely with Willow Creek, one of the largest evangelical churches in the country, to engage their leadership actively in advocating for immigration reform.

In 2011, World Relief and CLUE OC leaders with the support of the policy director of the National Association of Evangelicals began to work with the National Immigration Forum to organize the National Evangelical Immigration Table.[3] The Table has circulated a statement advocating principles for immigration reform. This statement has been signed by the leaders of 150 major moderate and conservative evangelical organizations, including Focus on the Family. On June 12, 2012, the Table held a press conference in the Senate building. Three days later, President Barack Obama gave an executive order to provide administrative relief for DREAM Act youth. There is evidence that the Table's actions gave the president the political cover that he needed in order to take this step.

The Table continues to create opportunities for dialogue and coordination as well as to support the expansion of grassroots organizing efforts in evangelical congregations and institutions around the country. The Table has demonstrated another contribution that the faith community can make to the broader effort for immigration rights and immigration reform: bridging and overcoming the partisan divide that often blocks positive legislation on immigration. The faith community does not narrowly fit within partisan boundaries but rather is one of the few (perhaps the only) institutions in our country that includes leaders across the political spectrum and creates common ground.

As these evangelical organizations and their efforts show, the faith community has already had an impact on immigration policies and reform measures. Rich Stearns, president of World Vision and a Table member, has said that immigration is one of the central civil rights issues of the twenty-first century.[4] The faith community was significant in the civil rights movement of the twentieth century and may well turn out to be equally significant in this one as well.

NOTES

1. Ruth Melkonian-Hoover, "Evangelical Perspectives on Comprehensive Immigration Reform," *G92* (blog), December 5, 2012, http://g92.org/evangelical-perspectives-on-comprehensive-immigration-reform/. See also Ruth Melkonian-Hoover, "The Politics of Religion and Immigration," *The Review of Faith and International Affairs* 6, no. 3 (2008): 25–31.

2. Matthew Soerens and Jenny Hwang, *Welcoming the Stranger: Justice, Compassion and Truth in the Immigration Debate* (Downers Grove, IL: InterVarsity Press, 2009); and M. Daniel Carroll R., *Christians at the Border: Immigration, the Church and the Bible* (Grand Rapids, MI: Baker Academic, 2008).

3. For more information on this organization, see their website http://www.evangelicalimmigrationtable.com.

4. Rich Stearns, personal communication with author.

TEN

Bridging Academia with Community

Rafael Luévano

In his keynote address at the conference, Rafael Luévano, a professor and Catholic chaplain at Chapman University, provided an insightful and personal perspective about the need to bridge academia with local communities. With scholars, community and religious leaders, and immigrants in the audience, the conference, as he noted, was a major starting point in realizing the benefits of public sociology in discussions related to immigration.

It is only a few blocks from my apartment at Holy Family Cathedral to Chapman University, but that short span of Lemon Street is more than enough to expose the separation between the worlds of academia and local community. As I pull out of the church parking lot, I see the differences already on that first block. On my right there are rows of modern apartments filled with Chapman students, while on the opposite side of the street there are small, low-income houses populated mostly by Latinos/as. At the end of the block, I see Mari Carmen, a stooped old woman wearing an Angels baseball cap, ragged sweatshirt, and baggy jeans. She is having a good day, her baby stroller helping her cart along huge, bulging bags of tin cans and recyclable plastic. I see her three or four times a week—and of course at Sunday Mass. I always wonder how long she can continue on.

As I wait at the eternal red light at Chapman Avenue, I see Omega Burger, filled with immigrants. At the bus stop, I spy familiar Latinas, many mothers juggling grocery bags and crying children, next to a group of Latino men in jeans and cowboy hats that make them seem somehow out of place. Finally the green light permits me to pass, and I reach Walnut Avenue, where I gaze at a long row of houses extending all the way down Lemon. On the feast of Our Lady of Guadalupe and Corpus

Christi, I process with the Latino community down the center of this street, pausing at various houses, so *el padrecito* can bless the altars constructed in front of the homes for grand feast days. I know the people on this street. Although I offer only part-time ministration at Holy Family Cathedral, they are my parishioners. These hundreds of Latinos/as pack the cathedral for Sunday Mass. I bless their marriages, I baptize their children, I anoint their heads with holy oil when they are sick or dying, I bury their loved ones, and I hear their confessions. I know their secrets. Most of these people are immigrants, and the vast majority of them undocumented.

I turn right on Walnut, cross Glassell, and then descend into the cavernous Lastinger parking lot below the university football field. I get out of my car and ascend to the university's main plaza, a pristine space bound by modern structures and manicured foliage. It is a sunny day, a lovely day, and students stroll across the plaza in loose, sporty, sometimes scanty California-style clothing.

I am privileged to serve as a priest, Catholic chaplain, and professor in the Religion and English Departments at Chapman University. I lecture on St. Augustine's conversion and engage students with the "dark night" of John of the Cross's mysticism; I unfold Genesis and Exodus and guide them through the Gospels. I introduce them to U.S. Latino theologians, such as Virgilo Elizondo; I watch them become transfixed by the Marxist influence of liberation theologians like Gustavo Gutiérrez.

As I cross this plaza, the same thoughts always churn in my head. My entire life might be summed up by the dichotomy on display during my brief commute here. I can see the towers of St. Joseph Hospital, where I was born right here in Orange, California. I was ordained thirty-one years ago at Holy Family Cathedral. I teach at Chapman. I enjoy a life of privilege. Yet I am so distant from my immigrant fellow residents. And I cannot forget that in 1927 my father paid a coyote eight dollars to lead him illegally across the border toward a dream of a better life for himself and his family.

In truth, I wonder how many in my university community are aware of what lies beyond the grand entryway, that pulsating Latino reality all of my colleagues must pass on the way to the parking lot. And does it ever occur to the Latinos/as of Lemon Street to cross that invisible boundary and enter the Chapman University campus? For me the questions seem to demand that we consider what responsibility the academic community has for the Latino community in our midst.

PUBLIC AND PROFESSIONAL SOCIOLOGY

My personal and professional struggle to integrate the ivory towers of academia with the grassroots reality of the local Latino community is not mine alone. And the distance separating these two communities is far more complex than I can fully unfold in these remarks. But for our present purposes, I believe my point is clear: to pose questions regarding the "public role" of academia, particularly concerning the social sciences—economics, political science, anthropology, geography, history, and even political ecology. And as we pose these questions this evening, we must be mindful that Chapman University's Sociology Department is the primary host of this conference. Thus we engage these questions' inherent tension from a sociological perspective on what is articulated as the distinction and interaction of "professional" or "academic sociology" and what is referred to as "public sociology."

Sociology is about society, about everyday events, which is to say, it is about us.[1] Sociology attempts to understand society. To be a legitimate "science," sociology must rely on peer-reviewed research and data collection. Unfortunately, these scientific processes and their goals at times leave professional sociology out of touch with the very society that it attempts to understand. But when communities exist outside the focus of the academic discipline of sociology, what value to those communities are academia's knowledge, sophistication, methodology, analysis, and quantification?

Cognizant of this disparity, Berkeley sociologist Michael Burawoy beckons the revitalization of the sociological discipline. Burawoy wants sociology to return to its roots, so to speak, by heralding what is referred to as "public sociology." Since his 2004 ascendancy to the presidency of the American Sociological Association on a platform of public sociology, the phrase has received broad attention. In a nutshell, Burawoy states that "public sociology brings sociology into conversation with publics, understood as people who are themselves involved in conversation. It entails, therefore, a double conversation."[2] Furthermore, the critical mass in the community should be able to use and benefit from the knowledge that is generated in academia.

The genesis of public sociology, at least in more recent times, descends from C. Wright Mills, who in 1959 referred to American sociology's tendency to insulate itself from the social reality, whether through building systems, abstract empiricism, or survey research. Current public sociology seeks to move beyond abstractions and engage the public directly. And rather than being limited to a particular method, theory, or set of policy values, public sociology is understood as a sociological way of engagement or style of conducting inquiry. Such study is grounded in the community; it engages real people.

This does not mean that we can do away with professional sociology. We must understand that professional and public sociology maintains a tense rapport, which Burawoy labels "antagonistic as well as interdependent." He notes that "they are antagonistic because they are accountable to different norms and audiences. They are interdependent because public sociology requires the input of professional sociology. [Professional sociology] depends on the interjection of relevancy and new ideas from [public sociology]."[3]

Burawoy proposes that the means to bridge this interdisciplinary disparity is to initiate various levels of debate—for example, over public policy, political activism, the purpose of social movements, or the institutions of civil society. Public sociology also establishes dialogue with professional sociology as well as dialogues within publics about their own communities. "As a mirror and conscience of society," Burawoy writes, "sociology must define, promote and inform public debate about deepening class and racial inequalities . . . environmental degradation, market fundamentalism, state and no-state violence. I believe the world needs public sociology—a sociology that transcends the academy—more than ever."[4]

What I find most fascinating and hopeful about public sociology is that this debate and dialogue is not just about what is or what is not in society, but about what might be. Public sociology is visionary. It seeks to forge a future through conversations within broad audiences to learn and change. At this conference, we apply the means of public sociology to consider the specific topic of immigration. While there is no singular definitive definition of public sociology, two components remain fundamental: to establish mutual engagement between the academic community and the local community (for us, this means creating a "California public sociology"); and to foster debate and/or dialogue with those constituencies. I consider each of these components in turn.

THE LOCAL COMMUNITY: SOUTHERN CALIFORNIA

While research can be conducted anywhere, it is essential for all of us gathered here this evening to keep in mind the obvious: we are in California. The Golden State has long been considered exceptional, a bellwether for national change, whether social, political, or economic. For example, during the last twenty years, Silicon Valley has made an inestimable contribution to change that extends far beyond our borders and will into the international arena.

California in general, and Southern California in particular, abounds with immigrants. For the last 150 years, people have steadily moved into the region from various parts of the world. Industries in California attract immigrants from the Pacific, Mexico, and Latin America; the ports of Los Angeles and Long Beach are but one example of this influx. This region is a melting pot—right here, right now—and it simmers with such issues as sweatshops, languages, race, and the confluence of cultures.

Is California still at the vanguard concerning these issues? Frank Quevedo, a local Latino community leader, lobbyist, and vice president emeritus of Southern California Edison, believes that California has become "a schizophrenic mess," pointing out that on the one hand we have the DREAM Act, which is helping to pave a pathway to citizenship for many immigrants, while on the other hand, we have Los Angeles police cracking down on day laborers in local Southern Californian communities.[5] Many contend that it is precisely such contradictions that are indicative of where Southern California stands on immigration.

If public sociology is a conversation between academia and the community at large, then by its very nature it must be grounded locally. So our conversation here today must be a dialogue within both university campuses, like Chapman, and ethnic enclaves, such as Bristol Street in Santa Ana. We must create a Southern Californian variety of public sociology on immigration.

DIALOGUE

What do we want to transpire during this conference? To what do we aspire this evening? Dialogue. Burawoy and other promoters of public sociology encourage explicit public and political debate. We come together today in the hope of establishing an ongoing and comprehensive conversation between the academic and local communities. At first glance, this vision may appear to be a simple task, even an obvious one. But let us break it down. What do the two communities have to offer each other?

We begin within the academic community. Academics are specialists in particular fields. To broaden this discussion within the academic community, our conversation must be interdisciplinary. Thus this conference has assembled experts in sociology, religion, law, Chicano studies, education, and communication. With this bountiful mix we create a vibrant and informed interchange of knowledge as well as experience. The work of scholarship is to think, to analyze—and we are afforded the luxury of time to engage in such work. Academics can facilitate this conversation by creating a safe and welcoming environment in general, as well as by structuring conferences such as this one, where community members feel free to speak openly and directly to us.

What do community leaders and the people bring to our conversation? *Los líderes comunitarios traen a esta conferencia su experiencia, que ha sido formada en las calles de Orange, Santa Ana, y Costa Mesa. Debemos escuchar a aquellos que luchan por los derechos humanos en las cortes y a aquellos que combaten en las reuniones de ciudades. Queremos escuchar a aquellos que ofrecen sus servicios en los hospitales y cárceles. Sí, también nosotros—todos nosotros—podemos aprender todavía de los administradores y profesores de preparatoria y de escuelas superiores, que trabajan con estudiantes Latinos. Las experiencias de los sacerdotes y de su personal pueden informarnos del pueblo Latino al que sirven, talvez su trabajo pueda todavía inspirarnos. Sin embargo, es la misma gente—la masa—quienes traen a esta conferencia las experiencias únicas vividas. Yo creo que sus contribuciones tomaran la forma de historias. Sus narraciones personales, de familia y de comunidad que capturan las luchas y éxitos de la inmigración, relatos verdaderos y conmovedores que ofrecen un sueño americano fresco y de desarrollo urgente, como también de la pesadilla americana. Yo quiero decir que esta noche tenemos aquí presentes gente verdadera. Gente de la comunidad, que pueden y deben presentar sus casos. Queremos escuchar de parte de ustedes. Relaten sus historias, relaten sus historias.* Community leaders bring to this conference expertise forged in the streets of Orange, Santa Ana, and Costa Mesa. We must listen to those who argue in courtrooms and who battle in town meetings. We want to hear from those who offer service in hospitals and prisons. And all of us can still learn from grade school and high school administrators and teachers. The experiences of priests and their staffs can inform and inspire us yet further. But it is the people themselves—*la masa*—who bring their unique life experiences to this conference. I imagine your contributions will take the form of stories—your personal, family, and community narratives that capture struggles and success of immigration, true and moving tales that offer a fresh and urgent unfolding of the American dream, which is, for many, a nightmare. This evening we have among us not only academics but also "real" people. We want to hear from you. Tell us your stories, tell us your stories.

Our conversation consists of scholars; community leaders; and—perhaps most important—the people themselves, the subjects of our discussion. The ideas of scholars can be incorporated, but these ideas must also be questioned and challenged. By talking with each other, we all benefit. We must take resources from the university to the community and from the community to the university.

This year's conference has been on the broad—perhaps overly broad—topic of immigration. In the future, we hope to open up conversation—annually or even semiannually—on a variety of subjects, such as poverty, homelessness, labor, and education. The list, like the needs, is virtually endless. But we look forward to your feedback and suggestions regarding this conference, as well as those to come.

My task in this address to a general, as well as an academic, audience has been rather straightforward: to articulate what is public sociology and how it works, and to communicate the vision of the organizer of this conference. I hope that I have accomplished this task. I offer special thanks to all of you who are attending this conference. Thank you for crossing that bridge. Thank you for your presence and all-important contribution. Yet the real thanks this evening is offered to people, who for the most part, are not present at this conference. I offer this poem by essayist Richard Rodriguez entitled "Gracias," which appropriately expresses gratitude for all of the things that immigrants do for us.[6]

"GRACIAS"

Thank you for turning on the sprinklers. Thank you for cleaning the swimming pool. And scrambling the eggs and doing the dishes.

Thank you for making the bed. Thank you for getting the children up and ready for school. Thank you for picking them up after school.

Thank you for caring for our dying parents.

Thank you for plucking dead chickens.

Thank you for bending your bodies over our fields.

Thank you for breathing chemicals and absorbing chemicals into your bodies.

Thank you for the lettuce and the spinach and the artichokes and asparagus and the cauliflower, the broccoli, the beans, and the tomatoes and the garlic. Thank you for the apricots and the peaches and the apples and the plums and the melons and the almonds. And the grapes.

Thank you for the willow trees and the roses and the winter lawn.

Thank you for scraping and painting and roofing, and cleaning out the asbestos and the mold.

Thank you for your stoicism and your eager hands.

Thank you for all the young men on rooftops in the sun.

Thank you for your humor and the singing.

Thank you for cleaning the toilets and the showers and the restaurant kitchens and the schools and the office buildings and the airports and the malls.

Thank you for washing the car. Thank you for washing all the cars.

Thank you for your parents, who died young and had nothing to bequeath to their children but the memory of work.

Thank you for giving us your youth.

Thank you for the commemorative altars.

Thank you for the food, the beer, the tragic polka.

¡Gracias!

NOTES

1. I base my reflection on Michael Burawoy's work. Michael Burawoy, "The Public Sociology Wars," *Handbook of Public Sociology*, ed. Vince Jeffries (Lanham, MD: Rowman & Littlefield Publishers, 2009), 449–74; Michael Burawoy, "A Public Sociology for California," *Critical Sociology* 34, no. 3 (2008): 339–48, esp. 341; and Michael Burawoy, "For Public Sociology," 2004 presidential address for the American Sociological Association, *American Sociological Review* 70 (2005): 4–28.

2. Burawoy, "For Public Sociology," 7.

3. Burawoy, "A Public Sociology for California," 341.

4. Burawoy, "For Public Sociology," 4.

5. Frank Quevedo, personal communication with author.

6. I offer my "gracias" to Rodriguez and Georges Borchardt Inc. for permission to publish his poem. "Gracias" was originally published by NPR.

Conclusion

Victoria Carty

As this book goes to press, the United States Congress is once again debating major immigration reform. The newly proposed legislation, if it passes, will have significant consequences not only for immigrants but also for American society as a whole across social, political, and economic dimensions. Each of the chapters in this book in some way addresses the causes of immigration across the U.S.-Mexican border, the experience of migrants once they land in the United States, the importance of public opinion in framing the debate, or community activist groups' engagement with forms of collective behavior to resist the escalating anti-immigrant sentiment. These mobilization efforts operate at the local, state, and national levels.

The conference that was held at Chapman University in the spring of 2012 on public sociology and immigration, and this subsequent volume, served as an attempt to circumvent the polarized discourse that too often jeopardizes serious discussion and debate about immigration reform. The various disciplines represented in the panels provided a nuanced introspection into the complexities of issues related to immigration. The intent of both the conference and this collection was to get around much of the confusion that surrounds entrenched beliefs about the pros and cons of immigration reform, and to expose the conflation of unrelated topics associated with those who enter the United States legally or illegally.

The interdisciplinary nature that this book embraces is vital to any comprehensive understanding of issues that pertain to immigration. Most research on immigration has been undertaken by social scientists. However, we contend that there is a chronic need for input from grassroots community organizers, and also importantly, from theologians who work within the communities that they serve to make sense of the complexities of the contemporary issues immigrants face.

The theological and community-based perspectives provided by some of the authors push the field of immigration study specifically, and public sociology more generally, forward by offering a fresh and too often overlooked viewpoint of the *humane* dimension of being an undocumented person in the United States. As some of the essays illuminate, theology has much to offer to this vexing social issue. Social Catholic teaching has always emphasized a striving for the common good, which can only be attained by working in solidarity with the most expendable and exploited members of society, and by considering the plight of those most vulnerable to a host of injustices.

What is often missing when it comes to discussions of immigration is a context of broader issues as they relate to immigration that often serves as push factors. Rather, shortsighted views prevail that accuse people of crossing the border to take advantage of economic and social benefits. The reality, as this book argues, is much more problematic. When products cross the border with ease, but the people, many of whom make those very goods, face criminal charges if they attempt to do the same, there is something inherently unjust and callous about immigration policies whether they are economically or socially based. Likewise, with the increasing deaths of migrants attempting to cross the border, due to a lack of being able to meet their basic human needs in their home country or fleeing violence, we must understand that immigrants, though typically framed as the "problem," are a symptom of the very real structural economic and political problems that inhibit a sustainable livelihood for them in their place of origin.

While the rhetoric of proponents of anti-immigration policies is often stated as "illegal is illegal," this fails to acknowledge that many are crossing without proper documentation because of these structural issues. In the case of Mexico, it is the lack of sufficient work and a dwindling social fabric due to violence that serve as the main jettison for immigration flows. Therefore, promoting increasingly anti-immigration legislation, building fences to keep the "other" out, and militarizing the border will fail to curb cross border immigration, as has been made clearly evident.

What makes this book significant to the immigration debate is not necessarily the scholarly contributors, but rather the space that it secures for the voices of the faceless to be heard through direct or indirect testimonials. In other words, the voices of those who suffer most from the plight of anti-immigrant policies and attitudes are heard in these essays. Migrants are indeed the face of globalization, and this conference and the volume seek to give immigrants a human face. It is public sociology that lends itself to a holistic approach to address such social issues as immigration through an interdisciplinary embracement of the complexities of social problems in an attempt to promote social justice. Borrowing from C. Wright Mills, Antonio Gramsci, Edward Said, and Michael Burawoy, this book calls on social scientists to refrain from being "sociological bookkeepers" isolated in the ivory tower. This is a call to scholars to become public intellectuals who play an active role in the communities in which they reside and who realize that they have as much to learn as to teach.

Public sociology is not particular to the issue of immigration, but can be applied to an array of community issues that can broaden the dialogue between those in academia and citizens in the community. The result can be a policy-oriented strategy that is grassroots in nature and serves as a pedagogical outlet that fosters critical discourse outside of the confines of academia and steers clear of the overly prevalent "professional" model of the social sciences. These kinds of interdisciplinary endeavors, aided by scholars working in conjunction with grassroots organizations, can assist in pedagogical and practical efforts that perhaps make the academy once again relevant to the communities in which they are embedded.

Index

Contributing Authors

Harold "Biff" Baker is director of Advanced Solutions at ALEKS Corporation, producer of cognitive science systems for mathematics education. Previously he was on the Russian faculty at Oberlin College and the University of California, Irvine. Baker is a long-time parishioner at Episcopal Church of the Messiah, Santa Ana, California, where he is active in social justice ministries and manager of the social action and information network. He is currently writing a book on lesser-known historical, artistic, community, and spiritual sites in the Los Angeles area.

Ivy A. M. Cargile is an assistant professor at St. Norbert College in Americacn politics. Specifically, her research interests involve studying immigration, race and ethnic politics, and the intersectionality of race/ethnicity and gender in politics. She has coauthored articles on the framing effects on Latino immigrants as well as the acquisition of democratic values by Latinos in the United States. Cargile has taught classes on immigration policy, the U.S. Congress and the presidency, and women in politics.

Victoria Carty is associate professor in the Department of Sociology at Chapman University. Her research has focused on various aspects of social movements that include labor activism; the peace movement; student mobilizations; immigration reform, and the impact that new media has on contemporary social movement activity, the topic of the book that she is currently completing. Her articles have appeared in *Mobilization: The International Journal of Research in Social Movements, Protest, and Contentious Politics; Social Movement Studies: Journal of Social, Cultural and Political Protest; Sociological Perspectives;* and *Research in Social Movements, Conflict and Change.*

Chris Haynes is assistant professor in the Political Science Department at the University of New Haven. His research includes understanding the effects of empathy on public opinion on immigration, looking at the impact of ethnic media consumption on political knowledge, and examining Asian American linked fate. Presently he is involved in a book project on framing effects on public opinion on immigration. His recently published coauthored article in *Perspectives on Politics* serves as a prelude to this work.

Patricia Huerta is CEO/cofounder of Padres Unidos, a nonprofit organization that helps build successful communities by providing educational and support services to families. She earned her master's degree in

161

social work from California State University, San Bernardino, in 2000; served as senior social worker for the County of Orange for over ten years; and has over twenty-five years of experience working with Latino families in various facets. She is currently adjunct professor through the Extended Education/College of Educational Studies Community Collaboration Program at Chapman University and serves as an instructor for the St. Ignatius of Loyola Rules of Discernment workshop at St. Peter Channel Catholic Church.

Rev. Rafael Luévano is associate professor in the Religious Studies Department at Chapman University. He also serves as the university's Roman Catholic chaplain and has been a priest for thirty-two years through the Diocese of Orange, California. He is the author of *Woman-Killing in Juárez: Theodicy on the Border*, published by Orbis Books in 2012, focusing on the feminicides in northern Mexico, and is currently conducting research on narco-related violence in Mexico. Luévano teaches courses on Christianity, scriptures, and religion and the arts. For the past thirty years, he has served as the chair of the Luévano Foundation, honoring his deceased parents, which offers scholarships to Catholic grade school children.

Karina Macias is a council member for the city of Huntington Park, California, and associate coordinator with the Sisters of St. Joseph of Carondelet in the Justice Office. She holds a master's degree in international studies, and her research has focused on the current War on Drugs in Mexico, the Merida Initiative, and the increase of human rights violations. Macias has been a long-time advocate for comprehensive immigration reform that addresses deportations and the push factors of migration.

Jennifer L. Merolla is associate professor in the Department of Politics and Policy at Claremont Graduate University. Her research focuses on how the political environment shapes individual attitudes and behavior across many domains, such as candidate evaluations during elections, immigration policy, foreign policy, and democratic values and institutions. She is coauthor of *Democracy at Risk: How Terrorist Threats Affect the Public*, published with the University of Chicago Press (2009). Her work has appeared in such journals as *Comparative Political Studies*, *Electoral Studies*, *Journal of Politics*, *Political Behavior*, *Political Research Quarterly*, *Political Psychology*, and *Women, Politics, and Policy*.

Ally Noble graduated from the University of Redlands in 2005 with a bachelor of arts degree in sociology and a minor in Latin American studies. After spending one year volunteering and traveling throughout Peru and Puerto Rico, she earned the Education, Environment, and Community graduate certificate from IslandWood, through the University of Washington. Noble has since attended Antioch University's Center for Creative Change with a focus on environment and community. She is currently an Early Childhood Montessori teacher at Woodinville Montessori School, located in Woodinville, Washington.

Adrian D. Pantoja is senior analyst at Latino Decisions and professor in political studies at Pitzer College, a member of Claremont Colleges in Southern California. His research has appeared in numerous books and academic journals, including *Political Research Quarterly, Political Behavior, Social Science Quarterly, American Behavioral Scientist, Ethnic and Racial Studies, Journal of Religion and Society, Journal of Ethnic and Migration Studies*, and *International Migration*. Pantoja also worked as a researcher for the Tomas Rivera Policy Institute and consultant to the National Association of Latino Elected Officials; the California League of Conservation Voters; the legal firm Garcia, Calderon, Ruiz; and the Universidad de San Carlos in Guatemala. He has offered expert commentary on Latino politics to various national and local newspapers.

Caitlin Patler is a PhD candidate in sociology at the University of California, Los Angeles (UCLA). She is a National Science Foundation Graduate Research Fellow, a Ford Foundation Pre-Doctoral Diversity Fellow, and a UCLA Center for the Study of Women Paula Stone Legal Research Fellow. Her research analyzes how immigration status affects education, employment, and health among youth and their families. Her work also explores how immigrants experience and resist exclusion in everyday life, within such institutions as schools and through detention and deportation policies. Patler's work is informed by over twelve years of activism in the Los Angeles immigrant rights community.

Rev. Edward Poettgen is pastor of Immaculate Heart of Mary Catholic Church in Santa Ana, California. He directs the mission of this large and vibrant parish through its evangelization teams, formation programs, liturgical celebrations, and service to the community. Poettgen has served for thirty-two years as a priest throughout Orange County among primarily immigrant communities. He is presently dean for priests in the Santa Ana churches; Episcopal vicar for charities; board member of Catholic Charities of Orange County, Orange County Community Housing Corporation, Comunidad Latina Federal Credit Union, and Interfaith Council of Central Orange County; and active volunteer with Orange County Immigrant Coalition and Orange County Congregation Community Organizing.

Rev. Alexia Salvatierra is currently director of Justice Ministries for the Southwest California Synod of the Evangelical Lutheran Church in America. She also consults with a variety of national/international organizations, including World Vision USA/World Vision International/Women of Vision, the Women's Donor Network, Auburn Theological Seminary, Interfaith Worker Justice, Sojourners, Intervarsity Christian Fellowship, and the Christian Community Development Association. She is an adjunct faculty member at the New York Theological Seminary and Biola University. She recently published a book on faith-rooted organizing through Intervarsity Press (2013). She has been awarded the Changemaker Award from the Liberty Hill Foundation; Stanton Fellowship from the Durfee Foundation; Amos Award from Sojourners; Giants of Justice Award from CLUE-LA (Clergy and Laity United for Economic Justice); and Prime Mover Fellowship from the Hunt Alternatives Fund.

Tekle M. Woldemikael is professor of sociology at Chapman University. His research interest involves immigrants and refugees, racial identity, ethnicity and nationalism, language, and public policy. He teaches courses on social theory, race and ethnic relations, and African society. He is author of the book *Becoming Black American: Haitians and American Institutions in Evanston, Illinois*, and is working on a book titled "The Invention of Eritrean National Identity." Woldemikael coedited a special issue of *The American Sociologist* entitled "Racial Diversity in Becoming a Sociologist." His articles have appeared in numerous journals and edited books. He earned his PhD at Northwestern University.